H in the Saddle

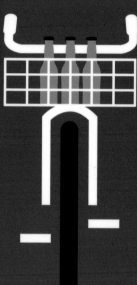

A Guide *to* Portland's Craft Beer Scene, *by Bike*

WRITTEN BY **LUCY BURNINGHAM** & **ELLEE THALHEIMER**
DESIGNED BY **LAURA CARY**

Praise for Hop in the Saddle

In a town bursting with bikes and beer, no one knows more about both scenes than writer Lucy Burningham. With her vast knowledge and experience surrounding the artisan bike culture and booming beer scene, Lucy has sipped, supped and cycled her way around Portland for years, noting her favorite meals, beers and bike paths along the way. Ride with Lucy and Ellee as they navigate you through the city's best of the best in this guide to Portland's food, drink and cycle culture."

MEGAN FLYNN | EDITOR AND PUBLISHER, *BEER WEST* MAGAZINE

"In Portland, I can't imagine a better pairing than biking and beer! Thankfully, three of the city's well-loved bike aficionados have made it easy for you to jump on two wheels, feel the wind in your hair, and skillfully navigate our system of bike boulevards that comprise our Platinum-rated Bicycle Friendly Community."

KRISTIN DAHL | SENIOR MANAGER OF DESTINATION DEVELOPMENT, TRAVEL OREGON

"Portland is loaded with so many beery destinations that even a longtime resident can become overwhelmed with options. Instead of taking a chance, follow Lucy to the choicest spots where the beer is top notch and the route is conveniently planned for you."

ALEX GANUM | FOUNDER AND BREWMASTER, UPRIGHT BREWING

"Portland is a mecca for many popular pursuits; chief among them, beer and biking. Lucy and Ellee's book captures the spirit of both of these with humor and adventure."

JASON FRENCH | CHEF AND OWNER, NED LUDD

DISCLAIMER

The content of this guidebook is purely for informational purposes and is intended as a reference guide. Hop in the Saddle, LLC and Into Action Publications, LLC and their respective employees, agents, representatives, and assigns, the authors and everyone involved with the creation of this book make no warranty of correctness or thoroughness and disclaim any and all liability resulting from its use, and no warranty is given that the information provided in this guidebook is correct, complete, and/or up-to-date.

Hop in the Saddle, LLC and Into Action Publications, LLC and their respective employees, agents, representatives, and assigns accept no liability whatsoever for any injury, damage, loss, accident, delay, or any other incident which may be caused by the negligence, defect, or default of any company or person referenced in this guidebook.

Hop in the Saddle, LLC and Into Action Publications, LLC and their respective employees, agents, representatives, and assigns are not liable for any bodily injury or harm, accidents property damage or personal loss as a result of, but not limited to: physical exertion; travel by any mode of transportation; consumption of alcoholic beverages; forces of nature, such as high winds, rain, excessive heat, etc.; heat exhaustion; equipment failure; civil unrest or terrorism; or the availability of medical services and the quality thereof.

Hop in the Saddle, LLC and Into Action Publications, LLC and their respective employees, agents, representatives, and assigns do not own or operate any entity which provides, or is to provide, goods or services referenced in this guidebook, including, for example, lodging facilities, transportation companies, food service providers, equipment suppliers, babysitters or daycare providers, etc.

HOW NOT TO GET DRUNK (DON'T GET DRUNK)

What's worse than hurting yourself because you're drunk on a bike? Hurting others. Here are our suggestions for avoiding irresponsible inebriation:

Dainty does it. Breweries will give small samples of beer to customers and "flights" of small tastes. Consider sharing these with a friend.

Eat a lot. Consuming calories, especially food high in carbohydrates and fat, while sampling beer will go a long way to help you stay on the straight and narrow.

Drink water. Sip your brew in micro-quantities, savoring and noting the flavors and experience. Then pound water.

WHOOPS, YOU GOT DRUNK

Cab services in Portland are accustomed to transporting bikes (and drunk people). Just let them know you have a bike when you call. Try **Broadway Cab** (*broadwaycab. com*, 503-333-3333), which uses hybrid vehicles. Or use **TriMet** (*trimet.org*, 503-238-7433), the area's extensive, easy-to-use public transportation system. All TriMet buses and MAX trains accommodate bikes on a space available basis.

SIT BACK AND ENJOY THE RIDE

Want to experience Portland's brew scene by bike but without worrying about your limits? Portland's pedicabs will take you and one or two friends on whatever tasting tour you desire.

Rose Pedals (*rosepedals.com*, 503-421-7433)
PDX Pedicab (*pdxpedicab.com*, 503-828-9888)
Portland Pedicabs (*portlandpedals.com*, 503-329-2527) ❀ COUPON! (*pg 4*)

H🏐P
in the
Saddle

A Guide *to* Portland's
Craft Beer Scene, *by Bike*

WRITTEN BY **LUCY BURNINGHAM** & **ELLEE THALHEIMER**
DESIGNED BY **LAURA CARY**

**INTO
ACTION**
PUBLICATIONS

Published in the United States by Into Action Publications, LLC. For information about the book, sales or speaking engagements, visit *intoactionpublications.com* or email *info@intoactionpublications.com*

1. Food & Drink   2. Regional: West   3. Travel

ISBN: 978-1621066033

Printed in the United States of America

Book Design: Laura Cary

First Edition

Cheers!

Cheers to our husbands! Thanks to Tony Pereira and our son Oscar for their patience, laughter and research assists. ♥ Lucy. Thanks to Joe Partridge for always helping me do the best I can, sacrificing your time to make this project happen and cheering me on when I need it. ♥ Ellee. Thanks to Michael Berg and our son Calder for the boundless mental and physical support, tolerance of my inner night owl and encouraging hugs. ♥ Laura

Huge kudos to the passionate brewers in this town who make good beer; the PDX bicycle lovers, movers and shakers; an amazing community of friends and family who gave us encouragement with every smile, applause and cheers as we created Hop in the Saddle; our backers on Kickstarter; Portland, for being Portland; Jeff, for his map-wizardry; Jess Gibson, for being our paparazzi for a day; and to Russ Roca of Path Less Pedaled, Team Beer, Rebecca Pearcy of Queen Bee Creations, Angie Hill of PixelKnit, Ben Greensfelder, Megan Flynn, Jason French, Alex Ganum, Alia Farah, Danielle Strom, Leah Nash of Leah Nash Photography, Metrofiets, Elly Blue, Pereira Cycles, Donnie Kolb and Lindsay Kandra.

Finally, big love to each other, for friendship, professional growth and for standing by one another every step of the way. Here's to craft beer, riding into the sunset and a damn good time.

Table of Contents

Let's Roll!

This book was designed to maximize your love of craft beer and cycling in Portland, quadrant by quadrant. Here's how: cruiser-friendly BEER ROUTES connect the RIDE STOPS, our favorite beer hot spots. We include some BONUS STOPS, more beer destinations within walking distance of RIDE STOPS. Bike parking is listed in the PARK IT boxes along with outdoor seating options, so you can keep an eye on your bike. Every chapter has a NIBBLES pick, the cream of Portland's food scene, plus a TO GO section, each quadrant's best bottleshop. EXTRAS are just that: great bars, nuggets of history, bike- and beer-centric lodging, and more. If you're itching for more cycling, look to the BIKE NERD EXTENDED ROUTES, which are conveniently connected to the BEER ROUTES and vary in difficulty. FYI, bike odometers vary, so don't freak out if cue mileages differ slightly.

Tell us about your adventures and let us know about any updates! *cheers@hopinthesaddle.com.*

BEER ROUTES
The city's primo bicycle boulevards and bikeways connect our favorite places to drink craft beer and chow down.

BIKE NERD EXTENDED ROUTES
Connected to the beer routes, these loops and out-and-back rides represent some of the best road riding from Portland proper.

DETAILED CUE SHEETS
Easy-to-read directions accompany all maps and include mile markers, warnings, instructions and beer stops.

BREWERIES
In a town bursting with craft beer, we've only highlighted breweries and brewpubs with noteworthy taps and cool vibes.

BOTTLESHOPS
We included our favorite speciality shops with extensive bottle selections. Some have attached tasting rooms.

BARS AND RESTAURANTS
We filtered the choices. Our priorities? Innovative cocktails, delicious nibbles and budget-friendly happy hours.

5 Beer Routes

20 Breweries

5 Bike Nerd
Extended Routes

8 Bottleshops

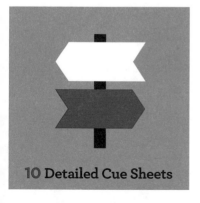

10 Detailed Cue Sheets

31 Bars and Restaurants

Hop in the Saddle
Highlights

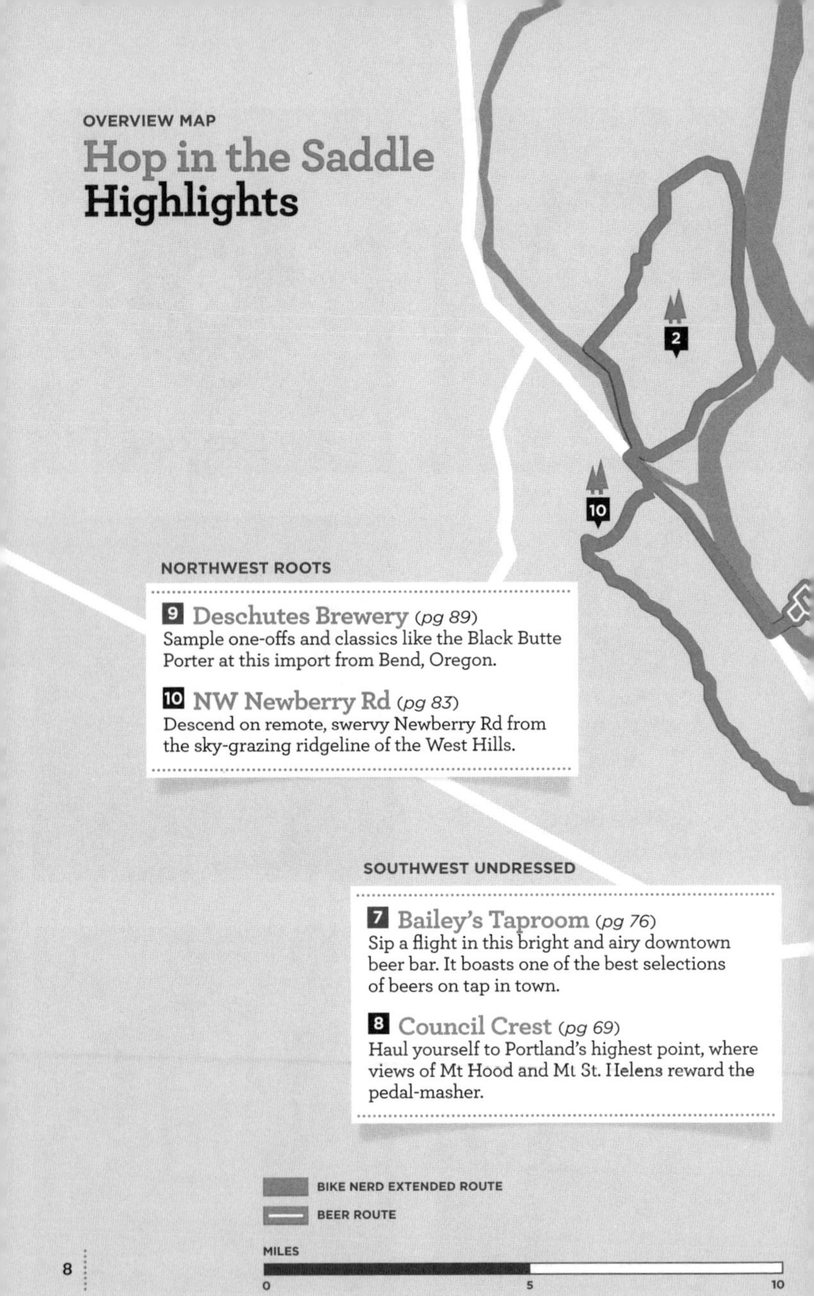

NORTHWEST ROOTS

9 Deschutes Brewery (*pg 89*)
Sample one-offs and classics like the Black Butte
Porter at this import from Bend, Oregon.

10 NW Newberry Rd (*pg 83*)
Descend on remote, swervy Newberry Rd from
the sky-grazing ridgeline of the West Hills.

SOUTHWEST UNDRESSED

7 Bailey's Taproom (*pg 76*)
Sip a flight in this bright and airy downtown
beer bar. It boasts one of the best selections
of beers on tap in town.

8 Council Crest (*pg 69*)
Haul yourself to Portland's highest point, where
views of Mt Hood and Mt St. Helens reward the
pedal-masher.

BIKE NERD EXTENDED ROUTE

BEER ROUTE

MILES

0   5   10

THE GREAT NORTH

1 Saraveza *(pg 29)*
Check out this beer bar and bottleshop, where the pomp of a Victorian parlor mingles with the vibe of a Midwest rec room.

2 Sauvie Island *(pg 21)*
While riding this flat island loop, stop to smell the lavender and shove fresh berries in your face.

NORTHEAST MASHUP

3 Breakside Brewery *(pg 43)*
Park your bike under a garden roof and sip an Aztec Ale, which blurs the line between beer and food.

4 Blue Lake Regional Park *(pg 37)*
Stake out your picnic spot after riding the Marine Dr Bike Path along the expansive Columbia River.

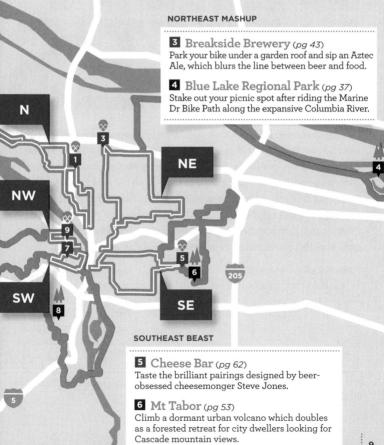

SOUTHEAST BEAST

5 Cheese Bar *(pg 62)*
Taste the brilliant pairings designed by beer-obsessed cheesemonger Steve Jones.

6 Mt Tabor *(pg 53)*
Climb a dormant urban volcano which doubles as a forested retreat for city dwellers looking for Cascade mountain views.

THE BIG PICTURE

BEER+
BIKES

Portlanders are spoiled. Our beer culture requires excellent and innovative brews. And our bicycle scene revolves around one of the most progressive cycling infrastructures in the country, internationally-recognized bicycle industries and motley bike fun. Individually, these beer and bike worlds set trends and distinguish the city. But the trailblazing doesn't stop there. In Portland, craft brew and bicycle cultures intertwine, soaking and stoking each other to inspire creativity and passion.

SWILLING AFTER SPINNING

While the scientific community has yet to conduct a proper inquiry, we, the authors, have conducted our own studies. Drinking beer after a bike ride is perfection. There's a reason mountain bikers stock their cars with coolers of beer instead of Manhattan fixings. While beer may not offer the same replenishment of, say, protein powder, a tasty brew offers distinct psychological benefits. Ask a bike messenger chugging a happy hour PBR or a cyclocross racer who reaches for a beer and a cowbell after the last lap. Beer offers its own flawless formula for recovery.

Photo: Jose Sandoval

OUR TOWN

Bike riding and beer drinking have a long unofficial history in Portland, but we can pinpoint some early beginnings. In 1896, the Portland chapter of the League of American Wheelmen built the city's first bicycle path to more easily access their favorite bar. Almost a century later, as Portland's craft brewing pioneers began to hang their shingles in the city's Northwest quadrant, the city elected a bike-loving mayor named Bud Clark (who was running a bar at the time, *see page 75*). As the city's bicycle infrastructure evolved, bike boulevards and lanes began connecting the ever growing network of breweries and world-class beer bars around the city.

CROSSOVER

Bikes and beer overlap in hundreds of ways here, from valet bike parking at the Oregon Brewers Festival to professional brewers who change out of rubber boots into cycling shoes at the end of the day. More profoundly, these two worlds energize each other because they're both fueled by passionate people who value quality of life. You know, beer aficionados who seek out the perfect locally brewed oyster stout, framebuilders who take the time to make a cargo bike to carry kegs of beer, and pub owners who beg the city to install bike corrals.

Tap into Brewtopia

Whether you call it Beervana or the City of Roses, Portland boasts a vast and varied beer scene. Like the city itself, Portland's beer world feels smaller and friendlier than one might expect. In this book, we've gone a step farther to help you tap into the beer scene by including only our absolute favorite places to drink craft beer and eat top-notch nibbles, from Euro-style cafes with a rotating cask tap to big-name breweries with small-batch beers. Welcome to paradise.

THE HISTORY
In 1887 Henry Weinhard, who was running a brewery in what is now the Pearl District, floated the idea of pumping beer from the brewery through fire hoses to the new Skidmore Fountain for its dedication ceremony. Even though city leaders firmly rejected the frothy idea, the proposal foreshadowed the future. Eventually Portland became a craft beer epicenter, starting in the 1980s when a handful of brewers opened some of the country's first commercial craft breweries.

THE CULTURE
In Portland, fiercely loyal people go out of their way to support local businesses, especially breweries. Most neighborhoods have at least one brewery, which translates to super fresh beer made nearby.

Portlanders take their beer seriously, and for good reason. During the dark wet days of winter, cheery brewpubs sustain locals by pouring hoppy IPAs and adventurous one-offs made with everything from lemongrass to bacon. But beer is more than just a way to relax and savor strange flavor profiles, it's what binds a community whose ranks include

HOP HEAVY
Hops only grow in a few places in the world, including the Pacific Northwest. The ingredient's locality may have inspired the ubiquitous Northwest-style India Pale Ale, a typically bitter beer with some combination of citrus, pine, grassy and floral notes.

LOCAL FOLK
Portlander **Fred Eckhardt** wrote the seminal "The Essentials of Beer Style" in 1989, and has gone on to become a widely respected beer writer and educator.

"It's not the beer, it's the beer," mused **Don Younger**, who once owned the **Horse Brass Pub**. Don passed away in 2011 and is missed for his koan-like phrases and unabashed beer drinking. He's toasted at almost every major Portland beer event.

"People ask me, Fred, what's your favorite beer? And you know what I say? The beer in my hand."

– FRED ECKHARDT –

bloggers, bottleshop owners, homebrewers and festival organizers. You'll undoubtedly encounter this tightly knit crew around town. Tell 'em we said hi.

TASTING TIPS

No one needs a primer on how to drink beer, but consider a few tips on how to better appreciate this fermented libation. First, slow down. Look at your beer—the quality of its head, the amount of carbonation you see in the glass. Then smell it. Does it remind you of anything (besides the fact that you're thirsty)? Now take a sip. How does the beer feel on your palate? Is it spiked with bubbles,

or smooth and creamy? How do the flavors change as you continue to sip? Is there an aftertaste? Most supremely: Do you like it?

We highly recommend trying a sampler tray at any brewery. It's a chance to taste a range of beers, which usually includes a seasonal and some styles you might not order otherwise.

OREGON BREWERS FESTIVAL
Beer lovers come to the OBF from all over the world to sip their way through more than 100 offerings at **Portland's Waterfront Park** during the last full weekend in July. Join the tens of thousands of people who roar with spontaneous group cheers all weekend long.

MUST-READS
Check out our favorite PDX beer blogs and resources:

Beervana
beervana.blogspot.com

Brewpublic
brewpublic.com

The New School
newschoolbeer.com

It's Pub Night
its-pub-night.com

Portland Beer
portlandbeer.org

The Beer Goddess
beergoddess.com

Oregon Brewers Guild
oregonbeer.org

The *Oregonian*'s The Beer Here
blog.oregonlive.com/ thebeerhere/index.html

Portland Taplister
portland.taplister.com

THE BIG PICTURE
Biketown, USA

All wheels point to Portland. The platinum-level bike infrastructure receives accolades, and the city's bicycle culture attracts widespread attention for film festivals, costume-crazed cross racers and die-hard commuters. But you'll only understand Portland's bike magic from the saddle. That's why we crafted the ultimate routes—combinations of our favorite multi-use trails, bicycle boulevards and bike lanes—plus stellar longer spins.

THE HISTORY

There's no shortage of praise for Portland's bicycle achievements, but the city didn't arrive here overnight. A history of elbow grease and progressive, long-term investment shaped the city. In 1971, Oregon's Bicycle Bill allotted 1% of a fiscal year's highway fund to cycling and pedestrian infrastructure—an unheard-of amount, yet still a meager portion of the overall budget. In that same decade, the city tore down its waterfront highway and replaced it with a park that included a wide pedestrian/bike path, then killed an eight-lane highway project through the Southeast quadrant to redirect funding to light rail.

Eventually Portland's TriMet became the first major transit agency to put bike racks on buses. As bikeway miles grew and cycle commuter rates increased, bike crashes decreased and infrastructure, including bike corrals, bike boulevards and green boxes, popped up all around town. The trend grows stronger everyday.

THE CULTURE

Ask any PDX cyclist to define this city's cycling culture and prepare for vociferous opinions and passionate Italian-style gesticulations.

PEDALPALOOZA
This three-week festival in June features around 300 community-created themed bike rides and events. **Fake Mustache Ride**, anyone?

"THE" BICYCLE SITE
Read the best news about PDX bicycle culture and transportation on *bikeportland.org*.

WHITE BIKES
Noticing white bikes chained to signs? "**Ghost bikes**" are placed where cyclists died as a result of car crashes. They exist to remind us of cyclists' right to safe travel. *ghostbikes.org*

WELCOME
PDX Airport welcomes cyclists. It has a bike assembly station near the MAX stop, bike parking, a tool checkout library and a multi-use trail leading to **Marine Dr Bike Path**.

Though the World Naked Bike Ride may get more attention, Portland's wholesome bike commuters are the cycling heart of this town.

The myriad of cycling subcultures, from track racing to bike polo, evade tidy summation. But one constant holds true: Portland loves bicycles. Robust "bike fun" includes freak bikes—both tall and fur-covered—and the infamous Zoobomb, a late-night, West Hills descent on mini bikes. More-athletic pursuits include the Wednesday evening racing series on Mt Tabor—where you can watch national-level racers duke it out—and the annual mud-splattered cyclocross races in the fall. Costumed races, Pedalpalooza and the World Naked Bike Ride may get most of the attention, but never underestimate the wholesome bike commuters, who ride no matter what and are the cycling heart of this town.

BEFORE YOU GO

Grab a Portland Bureau of Transportation's bike/walk map, the best source of info about bike-friendly roads. The quadrant-specific maps show bike shops, public restrooms, water fountains and public art. Find a PDF at *portlandoregon.gov/transportation/218* or free paper copies at many bike shops and tourist information places around town. Another good choice is the citywide, waterproof *Bike There!* map available for $9 (*oregonmetro.gov/index.cfm/go/by.web/id=38177*).

Before your brewery tour, read up on the rules of the road in *Pedal Power: A Legal Guide for Oregon Bicyclists* by Ray Thomas (a free download from at *stc-law.com/bicycle.html*). We don't condone riding drunk, which is both dangerous and illegal. End of story.

RIDE OREGON
This **Travel Oregon** site includes bike travel tips and other bike-oriented info. *rideoregonride.com/resources*

MORE PDX BIKING TIPS
Want some other tips for navigating town? Try the *PDX by Bike* zine *pdxbybike.com*.

PDX BIKE RENTALS
Rent cruisers, road bikes, cross bikes for Forest Park, tandems, surreys, touring bikes, kids equipment and trailers. Prices range from hourly to day rates, $9–75. Visit *hopinthesaddle.com/resources* for more info. Some bike rental places include:

Waterfront Bicycles
waterfrontbikes.com/rentals

Portland Bike Tours
portlandbicycletours.com/portland-bike-rentals
✿ COUPON! (*pg 4*)

Kerr Bikes
kerrbikes.org

Sellwood Cycle Repair
sellwoodcycle.com/rentals

Pedal Bike Tours
pedalbiketours.com

It's the Willamette, dammit.

NORTH
The "fifth quadrant" may seem like the city's side dish, but its diverse beer scene and bike love bring the flavor.

NORTHEAST
Northeast's red-carpet bike infrastructure will lead you to a lederhosen-loving German chalet or a bike shop where drinking beer with your mechanic is de rigueur.

FIVE QUADRANTS

That's right, five.

Portland seems designed for the mathematically inclined. Two rivers, 10 bridges and four quadrants. Plus one, the "fifth quadrant." A bend in the north-flowing Willamette River inspired four to become five. Within each quadrant, dozens of neighborhoods have their own unique vibes.

The Willamette separates the city's west and east sides, and Portlanders usually identify with one or the other. A summer afternoon barbecue with a ferocious game of cornhole? Eastside. High-fashion window shopping and jumping on the streetcar to Powell's Books? Westside. But there's no need to choose one over the other—put some of those 10 bridges to use and you too can have it all.

SOUTHEAST
Let the other quadrants weep with envy. The Southeast is, by far, the most beer- and bike-saturated section of town.

SOUTHWEST
More daily commuter than freak bike jive, the Southwest boasts a number of classic, don't-miss swilling hot spots.

NORTHWEST
The Northwest holds the origins of craft brewing in Portland and the U.S. Here, bicycling is the sexiest way to get around.

THE GREAT NORTH

Go Forth to the North

North Portland is affectionately known as the "Fifth Quadrant," which makes it seem like an extra, a side of syrup to the other four quadrants' fried chicken and waffles. Because extras are often ignored, even the most intrepid cyclist or beer drinker might end up skipping a visit. That would be a shame because, in this case, the syrup brings the flavor.

North Portland has a mix of industrial and residential neighborhoods bordered by the Willamette River to the west and the Columbia River to the north. The area holds some of the city's more affordable real estate, which has lured many artists and young families into making NoPo home. Don't miss Mississippi Avenue's spread of shops, restaurants and food carts, or St. Johns, a neighborhood with old-school diners and a historic bike shop. Lucy's full disclosure: "I live in North Portland, and I'm proud of my quadrant's quirky and diverse beer scene, and bike love. Only here can you find the most bike-bedecked beer bar in town and a brewery that refuses to brew IPAs. That's right. You're in my hood now."

SPOKES
"One of my favorite spots to lock up my steed is Amnesia Brewing. And the Desolation IPA is… well, copacetic."

**JANIS McDONALD
ACTIVE TRANSPORTATION MANAGER | PDOT**

SUDS
"I'll tell you a secret: Mississippi and Over-look neighborhoods kill it with great food and craft beer at nice prices."

**SARAH PEDERSON
OWNER | SARAVEZA**

THE GREAT NORTH
Bike Lowdown

BEER ROUTE | 17.6 MILES, MOSTLY EASY

This route includes the Bike Corridor (*see below*), multi-use trails, thriving pockets of hip commerce, up-and-coming bike boulevards and the chance to ride alongside an ever-growing population of folks trading four wheels for two.

At the southernmost tip of North Portland, the bike route begins at **Upright Brewing** (*page 25*), a hidden brew-gem in the heart of a tangle of swooshing traffic arteries and veins.

To start, walk your bike on the sidewalk two blocks east to the source of the iconic, north-flowing **N Williams Ave "Bike Corridor"** (*see right*).

At *mile 1.9*, the route takes you on a quiet **N Albina Ave**, but if you want to ride through an enclave of thriving, hip Portland businesses, take **N Mississippi Ave** instead.

The six-mile trek to the **St. Johns neighborhood** is via **N Willamette Blvd** (*mile 3.3*), a high-use bike commuter shared roadway with fabulous views of the forested **West Hills** and **Willamette River**. FYI, traffic increases after N Rosa Parks Way.

The haul to St. Johns is worth the time, not only for the beer-gems, but also for **Cathedral Park** (which begs for picnics), the regal **St. Johns Bridge** (our favorite) and one of the oldest bike shops in town, **Weir's Cyclery** (*page 21*).

On **N Concord Ave** (*mile 15.3*), you cross over a super-cool spiraled bike bridge before passing **Overlook Park**. Hop onto **N Interstate Ave**, a lively bike artery frequented by commuters, that ushers you to the close of the ride loop.

BIKE CORRIDOR
Development has mushroomed in pockets of North Portland. This growth, and subsequent bicycle and car traffic, produced the proverbial stretch marks of the **N Williams Ave/N Vancouver Ave Bike Corridor**, one of the city's flattest, quickest north/south thruways. In the summer, about 4,000 bike commuters ride it each day, with cycle-loving businesses on **N Williams Ave** between **N Skidmore St** and **N Fremont St**.

BIKE BUSINESS
While on **N Williams Ave**, visit **Sugar Wheelworks**, a fabulous custom wheel builder; **Queen Bee Creations**, a local hand-crafter of panniers and bike bags; **Sweetpea Bicycles**, a custom bike builder; the **United Bicycle Institute**, where you can learn to weld bikes or basic maintenance; and **Hopworks BikeBar**, one of the bikiest beer bars around.

BIKE NERD EXTENDED ROUTE | 22.4 MILES, MODERATE | 500 FT GAIN

Just a hop, skip and a jump from Portland, Sauvie Island provides a bucolic isle retreat for city dwellers who want to tromp around pumpkin patches in the fall and stain their mouths with fat berries in the summer. After pedaling out of the city, greens seem gleamier and blues seem brighter on Sauvie. While spinning past apple orchards and fields of lavender on the 12-mile loop around the island, you'll glimpse snow-capped Cascadian volcanoes.

Sauvie Island Loop

RIDE GIST
A short stint on Hwy 30 brings you to a flat scenic island loop. **Moderate**.

PULL OVER
Captured by Porches Beer Bus on **Kruger's Farm**

BEST VIEW
Mt St. Helens over fields of lavender.
WORST VIEW
Collins Nude Beach

After crossing the **St. Johns Bridge** (which dangles from trippy heights), you only have to spend three miles on the trafficked but generously shouldered **Hwy 30** before crossing a bridge to **Sauvie Island**.

If you head north to start the loop around the island, you'll soon see **Kruger's Farm**, the site of a few fall cross races and the **Captured by Porches Beer Bus** (*mile 6.3*).

The 12-mile loop around the island is flat, but if the wind is kicking up, you might be in low-gear land.

Portlanders like to head to Sauvie on the weekend in their cars, as well as on bikes. For a low-traffic pedal, we suggest going during the week.

CLOTHING OPTIONAL
Do you disdain the constraints of a swimming suit and prefer unfettered dips? Sauvie has a nude beach, **Collins Beach**, on the northeast part of the island.

WEIR'S CYCLERY
Weir's Cyclery is one of the oldest bicycle shops in Portland. The shop opened in 1925 as a catch-all "fix-it" shop. Over the years it has grown and evolved to sell bikes and bike accessories, making this family-owned business the best St. Johns go-to spot for all things bicycle.

N BEER ROUTE
Cue Sheet

0.0 START From  **Upright Brewing**, take the sidewalk eastward on **N Wielder St** for 1.5 blocks (*so you don't cross traffic twice*)

0.1 LEFT N Williams Ave

1.2 CHEERS! 2 Hopworks BikeBar

1.3 LEFT N Shaver St

1.5 LEFT N Haight Ave

1.6 RIGHT N Beech St

1.9 CHEERS!/RIGHT 3 Amnesia Brewing/ N Albina St (*or N Mississippi St option*)

2.3 LEFT/CHEERS! N Skidmore St/11 Prost!

2.4 RIGHT N Michigan Ave (*jogging left at the T directly ahead*)

2.9 CHEERS!/LEFT 4 Saraveza/ N Killingsworth St *3.2-3.4 No bike lane and heavier traffic.

3.3 LEFT/RIGHT N Concord Ave/ N Willamette Blvd

4.6 LEFT N Rosa Parks Ave (*at bikes only turn*)

7.1 ALERT! Bike lane ends, wide shoulder

8.0 LEFT N Baltimore Ave (*steep hill ahead!*)

8.2 CHEERS!/STRAIGHT 5 Occidental Brewing Co./Entering **A Cathedral Park** and the multi-use path that goes under the bridge.

8.5 VEER RIGHT Towards the river; enter sidewalk of 'water pollution control laboratory' along river.

8.8 STRAIGHT Path spits you out onto the hill of **N Burlington Ave**

9.1 LEFT N Willamette Blvd

9.4 RIGHT N St Louis Ave

9.5 STRAIGHT Continue, crossing a trafficked road

9.6 RIGHT N Central St

9.8 LOOK! B St Johns Park

10.7 RIGHT N Gilbert Ave

10.8 LEFT N Lombard St (*can use wide sidewalk on bridge*)

10.9 RIGHT On multi-use path, to '**University of Portland**'

11.1 LEFT N Princeton St

11.4 LOOK! C McKenna Park

11.8 LOOK! D Portsmouth Park

12.2 LEFT/VEER RIGHT N Olin Ave/N Stafford St

12.5 RIGHT/LOOK! N Woolsey Ave/ E Columbia Park

12.6 LEFT N Willamette Blvd

13.2 LEFT/RIGHT N Wabash Ave/N Bryant St

14.1 RIGHT N Concord Ave

14.3 STRAIGHT through bike-only thruway, jogging back onto **N Concord Ave**

14.6 RIGHT/LEFT N Ainsworth St/N Concord Ave

15.3 LOOK! F Go over cork screw bike bridge

15.7 ALERT! N Concord Ave becomes **N Overlook Blvd**

16.0 RIGHT N Interstate Ave

16.7 RIGHT/STRAIGHT to '**N Russell St Eastbound**;' hooks around to **6 Widmer Brothers Gasthaus Pub**/Continue on **N Russell St**

17.2 RIGHT N Flint Ave

17.6 END Leftbank Building

EXTRAS:
7 Barrique Barrel
8 Fifth Quadrant
9 Interurban
10 Friendly Bike Guest House
11 Prost!
12 Hop and Vine
13 Weir's Cyclery

Pedaling along the bluffs of N Willamette Blvd.

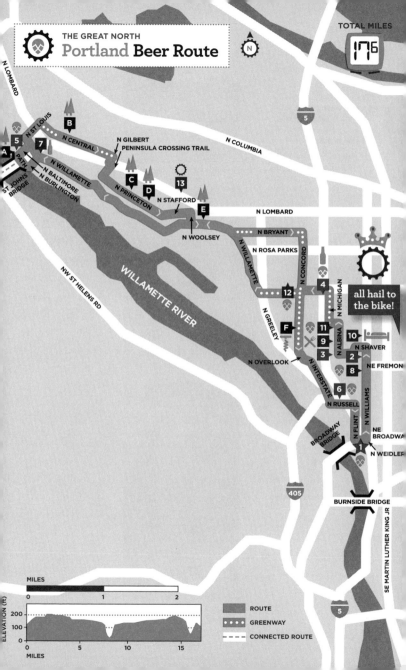

N EXTENDED ROUTE
Cue Sheet

0.0 START ★ From *mile 7.9* of the beer route on **N Willamette Blvd**, take a **RIGHT N Alta Ave** then an immediate **RIGHT N Syracuse St**

0.1 RIGHT onto the **St. Johns Bridge**. Take the sidewalk if you don't want to be in traffic

0.8 RIGHT off of bridge onto unsigned **NW Bridge Ave**, towards Hwy 30

1.2 LEFT Hwy 30, to 'Scappoose'

4.7 RIGHT over the **Sauvie Island Bridge**, to 'Sauvie Island'

5.1 Road becomes **NW Sauvie Island Rd**

6.3 BERRIES/CHEERS! Kruger's Farm on right, home to **1 Captured by Porches Beer Bus**

6.9 RIGHT NW Reeder Rd

8.1 VEER RIGHT continuing on **NW Reeder Rd**

11.2 RIGHT NW Gillihan Loop Rd

17.4 RIGHT Road intersects with **NW Sauvie Island Rd**; go back the way you came

22.4 END Enter **St. Johns** from the **St. Johns Bridge**

Off-roading on Kruger's Farm.

Photos: Meaghen Murphy

Picture perfect picnic spot at Cathedral Park beneath the St. Johns Bridge.

NW CORNELIUS PASS

NW SKYLIN

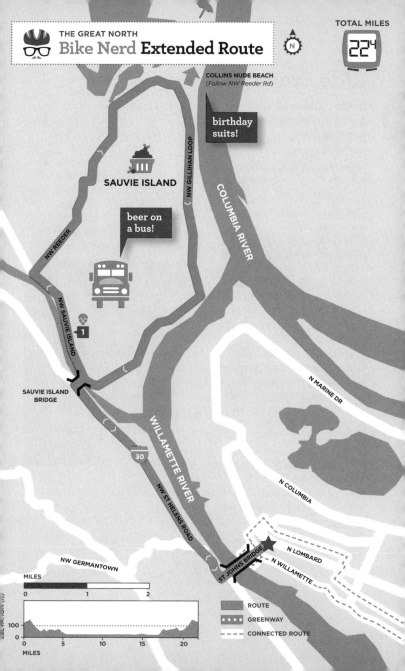

THE GREAT NORTH
Ride Stops

1 Upright Brewing
240 N Broadway, Suite 2
503-735-5337
uprightbrewing.com

HOURS: Fri 4:30-9pm, Sat-Sun 1-6pm,
BLAZERS HOME GAMES: 6pm-tipoff

The Upright tasting room is one of those secrets we'd rather keep to ourselves. After all, a little underground tasting room inside one of Portland's coolest, most innovative breweries could lose some of its charm if throngs of thirsty people showed up. But we're willing to take the risk because everyone should visit Upright at least once.

Brewer and owner Alex Ganum named the place after jazz musician Charles Mingus (and his upright bass). Alex wants his beers to reflect Mingus's style, by defying categorization but instantly expressing greatness. In most cases, he succeeds. We dare you to sip anything Upright while listening to *Mingus Ah Um* and not have a moment. The beers are Belgian and French farmhouse in style, but vary wildly, from the Fatali Four, a wheat beer overlaid with hot fatali peppers, to the oyster stout, one barrel of which was infused with Oregon black truffles.

Take your time in this little relaxed cavern, where beer ages in barrels and brews in steel. Play a board game or chat up other imbibers, most of whom will be Upright super fans who can tell you about their favorite releases and Alex's accomplishments.

PSST!
If you're lucky, you'll catch live blues music on a Sunday.

INSIDER SIP
Some of Upright's beers are named after numbers (**Four**, etc.) that correspond to each beer's "starting gravity," the amount of sugar in the beer before it ferments.

PARK IT
Bike staples pepper the perimeter of the **Leftbank Building** where Upright resides. No outdoor seating.

2 Hopworks BikeBar
3947 N Williams Ave
503-287-6258
hopworksbeer.com

HOURS: **Sun-Thurs 11am-11pm,**
Fri-Sat 11-12am | HAPPY HOUR:
Daily 3-6pm & 9pm-close

New to town? Come inside to see what makes our town so, well, Portland. The beer is organic, a rare trait for a craft beer. The Survival "7-Grain" Stout and Hopworks IPA are two classics, but don't pass up the chance to try special releases, like a Belgian strong ale or fresh hop blonde. All beer is brewed at the flagship HUB (Hopworks Urban Brewery) location in Southeast.

If you're unclear about how HUB feels about bikes, take note of the frames hanging above the bar, which were donated by local framebuilders. Then step onto the patio, and take a peek at what must be the largest bike rack ever installed at a pub (we're pretty sure it's longer than the bar). A few select sandwiches were designed to fit in your water bottle cage, and some come with a side 22 of HUB beer (again,

nice cage fit). If you'd like to show passersby on N Williams Ave how you can perform in the saddle, jump on one of the stationary bikes out front and get into time trial form. Each pedal stroke produces energy for the off-the-grid ecoFLATS building that houses the BikeBar.

Finally, delve one step deeper into Portlandia by ordering a vegan or gluten-free item off the menu before getting inked at the tattoo parlor next door.

BONUS STOP
Fifth Quadrant
3901 N Williams Ave
503-288-3996
lompocbrewing.com/
fifthquadrant_home.html

HOURS: **Mon-Thurs 11-12am,**
Fri-Sat 11-1am, Sun 11am-11pm
HAPPY HOUR: **Daily 4-6pm, 10pm-close**

Since you've already locked your bike to hit HUB, saunter over to the **Fifth Quadrant**, a classic Portland brewery in the same block. You heard us. The same block. As one of the **Lompoc Brewing** locations, the Fifth Quadrant brews delicious beers, including special barrel-aged ales available for tasting at the attached **Sidebar**.

PSST!
Every fall, Hopworks SE throws a **Bike to Beer Fest**, with live music, bike competitions (like BMX throwing) and plenty of beer.

INSIDER SIP
Hopworks is one of about a dozen breweries in the country to exclusively brew organic beers. Yes, it's a big deal.

PARK IT
Gargantuan bike rack around the back next to outdoor seating, bike staples in the front and a bike corral around the corner.

3 Amnesia Brewing
832 N Beech St
503-281-7708

HOURS: **Mon-Tues 3-11pm, Wed-Sun 12-11pm** | HAPPY HOUR: **Mon 3-11pm, Tues-Fri 4-6pm**

The outdoor patio at Amnesia always feels like a beach party, even on the bleakest rainy days. Maybe it's the communal picnic tables (some of which are covered by tents) or the fact that dogs are welcome to roam around the outdoor grill and nap on whatever piece of pavement suits their fancy. While we've never seen anyone throwing a Frisbee here, we're pretty sure that would be okay, too. Other things that are okay on the patio: smoking and lounging. Not okay: babies and kids.

This Mississippi Ave streetside pub was one of the first businesses on what was a run-down stretch a decade ago. It was an early anchor of what has become a prime destination for eating, shopping and drinking. The whole time, Amnesia has been brewing a solid lineup of classic Northwest beers in the pub attached to the patio.

If you catch Amnesia on a sunny day, kick back with one of the more sessionable, low-alcohol ales as you slather on some sunblock. Maybe you'll make some new friends and eat a brat topped with kraut. Don't expect things to happen in a hurry, however; you're at the beach.

PSST!
Watch for the occasional Amnesia event, including the **Single Hop Fest**, which features beers made with...you guessed it... just one kind of hop.

INSIDER SIP
The Copacetic is one of Portland's classic IPAs. Pours cloudy and orange, and tastes hop piney.

PARK IT
The sweet outdoor seating is right next to the bike corral.

4 Saraveza
1004 N Killingsworth St
503-206-4252
saraveza.com

HOURS: **Daily 11am-12pm**
HAPPY HOUR: **Mon-Fri 4-6pm**

This beer bar and bottleshop is a cross between a Victorian parlor and a 1970s rec room. While you won't find elaborate wallpaper or shag carpet here, Saraveza is a wonderfully dark and cozy space with high ceilings, vintage beer kitsch and bottle cap mosaics on nearly every horizontal surface. Bartenders toss wry jokes just as often as they share tidbits about what's on tap and why. To reach the bar, you must pass the large, glass-doored vintage coolers filled with a delicious range of bottled imports and fine American beers. Good luck staying focused.

On certain afternoons, you may find yourself among serious Cheeseheads, the kind who would rather talk Packers football instead of the merits of eating the washed rind of Taleggio. These imbibers help complete Saraveza's homage to Midwest awesomeness, which even shows up in the bar's food. Try one of the pasties—a version of the empanada—which are made of baked pastry dough folded over braised meats, potatoes and veggies. Or dig into some deviled eggs, pickled vegetables, Chex mix or a cupcake.

PSST!
The bar's moniker is a play on the owner's name. **Sarah Pederson** is one of the city's prominent women in beer, and she's in-house most days.

INSIDER SIP
Every second Monday of the month, slices of housemade bacon are free with every pour, but only if you ask.

PARK IT
Right outside there is a bike corral next to outdoor seating (and a burly meat smoker).

5 Occidental Brewing
6635 N Baltimore Ave
503-719-7102
occidentalbrewing.com

HOURS: **Wed-Thurs 4-7pm, Fri 3-8pm, Sat 12-8pm, Sun 12-6pm**

You will not find an IPA in the taproom of Occidental Brewing. I repeat, there are no IPAs. Not today, tomorrow or ever. That's because brewmaster Dan Engler only makes German-style beers, like the smooth Dunkel and hoppy Altbier. He figures the other 800 brewers in the Pacific Northwest have the hoppy IPA thing covered.

The brewery rests in the shadow of the great St. Johns Bridge, a beautifully imposing green Gothic-spired span. The taproom, on the other hand, is a modest square of space carved out in the corner of the echoey brewery, where a quilt-like montage of vintage beer cans hangs on the wall. Seasonal beers are always worth sampling, and the flight is a good way to become familiar with Occidental's interpretation of German brewing techniques.

Fill a growler and head down the hill to Cathedral Park, where you can watch boats cruise up and down the Willamette River and check out the underbelly of the bridge. But, if you choose to take a swig, don't blame us if you get busted for drinking beer in the park.

TO GO

Barrique Barrel
7401 N Burlington Ave
St. Johns
503-208-3164
barrelpdx.wordpress.com

HOURS: **Fri 12-9pm, Sat 12-8pm, Sun 12-6pm**

This recent addition to St. Johns fills a real neighborhood need—a place to get great bottles of everything from cider and sour beers to the best Oregon-made rosés. Owner **Lisa Lavochkin** can guide anyone through her carefully stocked shelves in this bright, airy space. But don't plan to do any tasting on-site; all bottles are sold to go.

PSST!
Occidental only brews with German-grown hops, which helps create beers that don't have the citrusy notes found in so many Northwest-sourced hops.

INSIDER SIP
The Dunkel is a light, bready beer with just the right amount of hoppy bite.

PARK IT
No official bike parking here, but you can prop your bike up outside the glass roll-up doors and keep an eye on it while you're in the tasting room.

6 Widmer Brothers Gasthaus
955 N Russell St
503-281-3333
widmerbrothers.com

HOURS: **Sun-Thurs 11am-10:30pm, Fri-Sat 11am-11pm** | HAPPY HOUR: **Mon-Fri 2-5pm**

Most likely you've heard of Widmer Brothers Brewing, which brothers Rob and Kurt Widmer opened in Portland in the 1980s when "craft beer" was as common as kimchee in the public's consciousness. What put Widmer on the craft beer map was their Hefeweizen, fitting for boys born to a German mother. But these days, the Hefe isn't what sets the brewery apart.

You'll smell what we're talking about as you bomb down the hill on N Interstate Ave, where the air becomes thick with the sweet aroma of grains roiling in hot water. The smell is pervasive because these days Widmer makes about 700,000 barrels of beer a year. That's a lot. The success of the staple beers has allowed brewers to experiment with a range of seasonals and one-offs. In the past year, some of Widmer's best beers were brewed with experimental hops.

Don't stop here for the food or the atmosphere, although the historic 1890 brick building adds some ambiance. Stop because the brothers are still steering this ship. If you want to pay homage to the deepest roots of Portland brewing, order a Hefeweizen, which always comes with a slice of lemon.

PSST!
The new brewing tanks across the street are so big they were installed by taking the roof off the building.

INSIDER SIP
Widmer is experimenting with gluten-free barley beers, using proprietary methods.

PARK IT
The double-parking space bike corral in front represents just one way Widmer supports the cycling community in Portland.

THE GREAT NORTH

❧ Extras

NIBBLES

Interurban
4057 N Mississippi Ave
503-284-6669
interurbanpdx.com

HOURS: **Mon-Fri 4pm-2:30am,**
Sat-Sun 10-2:30am, Sat-Sun 10am-2pm,
HAPPY HOUR: **Mon-Fri 4-5:30pm,**
Sun 10pm-close

Oh, the brooding you could do.
Hunker down under a glowing
Edison light bulb and mounted
deer head in this long, dark saloon
for some elevated pub food. Chef
John Gorham, of the famed Tasty
n Sons and Toro Bravo restaurants,
created a menu that makes you
want to drink the 12 beers on tap.
Beer-friendly dishes include bone
marrow with salsa verde, chicken
liver mousse, gourmet corn dogs,

shepherd's pie and a generous
charcuterie platter made up of
cured meats from local salumerias.
Don't miss the French toast sun-
dae, a decadent treat dripping with
caramel and sprinkled with nuts.

TO GO

The Hop and Vine
1914 N Killingsworth St
503-954-3322
thehopandvine.com

HOURS: **Bar: Daily 3pm-12am**
Bottleshop: Fri-Sat 11am-10pm,
Sun-Thurs 3-10pm

Originally a standalone bar with
a distinct Napa wine country
feel, the Hop and Vine added a
compact new bottleshop in the
space next door well after it had
established a local following.
While wine is prominently
showcased in the shop, owner
Yetta Vorobik loves beer, which
is why you'll find plenty of
special bottles. Drinking a beer
in the pub's backyard is like
hanging out in a friend's garden.
So open one of those bottles if
you just can't stand to wait.

Captured by Porches Beer Buses (multiple locations)
971-207-3742
capturedbyporches.com

HOURS: Varies, but usually open weekends only. Check website for details.

In case you never had the chance to drink beer while taking the school bus, Captured by Porches Brewing Company transformed a few of those old yellow buses into kitschy wheeled pubs. These school buses are decked out with board games and vintage furniture—cozy places to sit with a Mason jar full of Captured by Porches beer, which is brewed across the river in St. Helens. The buses tend to relocate, so check the website for updates. Current North Portland locations include St. Johns and Kruger's Farm on Sauvie Island.

Friendly Bike Guest House
4039 N Williams St
503-799-2615
friendlybikeguesthouse.com

RATES: Rooms $45-76, Bunk $36

Equipped with a mechanic stand and indoor bike lock-up, this hostel caters uniquely to bicycle tourists. Bonus: the hostel is located right on the North Portland Beer Route, within walking distance of Hopworks BikeBar and the United Bicycle Institute (*bikeschool.com*).

Prost!
4237 N Mississippi Ave
503-954-2674
prostportland.com

HOURS: Mon-Fri 11:30-2:30am,
Sat-Sun 11-2:30am

Step into Prost! and enter a world where beer is spelled "bier" and soccer is always called "football." The bar features German beers and nothing else. Sorry, locavores. Choose from classic Spaten, Paulaner and

Ayinger imports served in the same glassware you'd find in real German beer halls. Instead of ordering a pretzel or brat from the menu, expand your global scope in the adjacent food cart pod, which has a range of choices; Prost! welcomes beer-drinking patrons to carry in food from the carts.

NORTHEAST MASHUP

Riding the Red Carpet

Between the idyllic bungalows tucked into leaf-canopied bicycle boulevards and the bustling Lower Burnside zone, the Northeast holds a smorgasbord of beer and bike destinations. There's everything from a lederhosen-loving, German-themed chalet on Sandy Boulevard to a bike shop where you can drink beer with your mechanic, and a barbecue shack disguised as a bottleshop.

SPOKES
"Best part of NE? Aliens, smiley faces and batman symbols on the speedbumps on NE Klickitat, a fabulous bicycle boulevard."

**BARB GROVER
CO-OWNER | SPLENDID
CYCLES AND CARGO
BIKE EVANGELIST**

SUDS
"A patchwork of neighborhoods with pubs and breweries within walking or biking distance of each other keeps the people happy and tipsy!"

**BEN MEYER | CHEF
GRAIN & GRISTLE**

The Northeast rolls out Portland's red carpet bike infrastructure: from quiet neighborhood greenways to intersections equipped with bike-only crossings. As a result, bikes are respected as traffic, not just as a rebellious mode of transportation. In the same vein, Northeast locals take beer seriously by filling growlers and drinking pints at their neighborhood brewpubs, everywhere from Alberta Street to the Hollywood District.

NE

NORTHEAST MASHUP
Bike Lowdown

BEER ROUTE | 13.1 MILES, MOSTLY EASY

Without a doubt, bicycling has become a mainstream form of transportation with its own traffic veins and arteries, bike-specific signs and traffic lights, and "green bike boxes." This route flaunts some of the city's best cycling infrastructure, one tree-lined bike boulevard at a time. Bonus: you'll pass a micro park with public bike tools plus other green spaces that will make you pine for a picnic.

Check out the green bike box and bicycle-specific turning lane at **NE 12th** and **NE Lloyd Ave** (*mile .7*). Traffic filters remove cars from the **NE Tillamook St bike boulevard** (*mile 1.4*), and a multi-use path leads to **Irving Park** (*mile 2.6*).

Craftsman-era homes (lavish in a porchy, Portlandia way) flank wide, picturesque **NE 18th St** (*mile 1.5*), where you can practically hear Beaver Cleaver being called for dinner. Picnic opportunities abound at leafy **Irving Park** (*mile 2.6*) or **Wilshire Park** (*mile 7*).

At **Breakside Brewing** (*mile 4.4*), your bike can fit comfortably under the sidewalk bicycle shelter, which boasts a roof garden. Hello, Portland.

At *mile 4.7*, you can't miss the adorable **NE Holman and 13th Park**, which also serves as a vehicle sieve to prevent car traffic from entering the **NE Holman bike boulevard**. This crossroads provides bike staples, a picnic table and community board (check out the roof garden) with bike tools and a pump for anyone to use. Rad.

The stretches of bike boulevards between *mile 4.7* and *8.7* follow designated neighborhood streets. You can revel in the fact that this is your place and your street, because you travel by bike.

GAME ON!
Check out an intense game of **Hardcourt Bike Polo** in **Alberta Park** (**NE 22nd/Killingsworth**) on Sunday afternoons, battled out between bike messengers and their associates. (*portlandbikepolo.com*)

BIKE PLAYGROUND/PUB
A former bowling alley on the outskirts of Northeast Portland has been transformed into **The Lumberyard** (*lumberyardmtb.com*), a giant indoor bike park with jump lines, pump tracks, skill sections and technical trail riding for beginners to experts. Cherry on top? **The Pub @ the Yard** has local beer on tap and aims to serve locavore food. Gotta love Portland.

EXTENDED BIKE NERD ROUTE | 26.2 MILES, EASY-MODERATE | 410 FT GAIN

For those riders who wince at the thought of cycling up a hill, the Marine Dr Bike Path is for you. Flanking the Columbia River, this path meanders to Blue Lake Regional Park, where locals splash around and picnic their hearts out. For those looking to up the epic, keep heading east to the dramatic Historic Columbia River Highway.

Blue Lake Ramble

NE

RIDE GIST
This route is longer and flatter than the others. Wind may be your challenge. **Easy-moderate.**

PULL OVER
Cool off or picnic at **Blue Lake Regional Park**.

BEST VIEW
Marine Dr Bike Path skirts the scenic shores of the **Columbia River**.

The **Marine Dr Bike Path** (*mile 2.6*) is a multi-use trail next to the **Columbia River** used by all types, from in-line skaters to families poking along.

The path sometimes merges onto **Marine Dr**, a busy road, but there are generous bikes lanes.

Some pedal-mashers like to stick to **Marine Dr** to avoid the weaving **Marine Dr Bike Path** and also to steer clear of pedestrians and slower bicycle traffic (on weekends particularly).

On a blustery day, you will pray for the wind to be at your back.

At *mile 3.9*, you pass **Broughton Beach**, a sandy spot on the Columbia where people like to chill and swim on hot days. Warning: it's not the cleanest.

When you reach the picnic mecca of **Blue Lake Regional Park** (*mile 13.6*) you have the option of playing in the spray park or renting a paddle boat. Cheers to multi-sport endeavors!

UP THE EPIC
Marine Dr brings you to the gateway of the **Historic Columbia River Highway**. This roadway attracts the recreationally inclined, as well as cyclists who like to climb. An enormous vista of the **Columbia River Gorge** and surrounding unearthly landscape compensates the lactic acid burn of the climb to the **Women's Forum** (*25.2 miles from the beer route*). A unicorn rearing up and waving its mane would seem perfectly in place.

NE BEER ROUTE
Cue Sheet

0.0 START From **Burnside Brewing** head north on **NE 7th Ave**

0.1 RIGHT NE Davis St

0.3 LEFT NE 12th Ave

0.7 RIGHT NE Lloyd Blvd, becomes **NE 16th Dr** then **NE 15th Ave**

1.1 RIGHT NE Weidler St

1.2 LEFT NE 16th Ave (take crosswalk if it's easier to cross traffic)

1.4 RIGHT NE Tillamook St (*bicycle-only access*)

1.5 LEFT NE 18th Ave

2.2 LEFT NE Klickitat St

2.4 STRAIGHT Continue on multi-use path, crossing several streets

2.5 STRAIGHT Continue on path, entering **A Irving Park**

2.6 RIGHT on path past restrooms

2.7 STRAIGHT crossing **NE Fremont** onto **NE 9th St** (watch for curb)

3.3 LOOK! Look up to check out **B St. Andrew Church**'s gothic spire

3.5 STRAIGHT jogging to the right to follow **NE 9th Ave**

4.1 LEFT/RIGHT NE Holman St/NE 8th Ave

4.4 RIGHT/CHEERS!/VEER RIGHT NE Dekum St/ 2 Breakside Brewing/ NE Durham Ave

4.7 VEER LEFT/LOOK! Following **NE Holman St** through bicycle thruway/ **C NE 13th and Holman Park**

4.8 STRAIGHT Continue on **NE Holman St** following bicycle blvd symbols

6.0 RIGHT/LOOK! NE 37th Ave/ D Fernhill park

7.0 LOOK! E Wilshire Park

7.4 STRAIGHT JOGGING LEFT road becomes **NE Alameda St**

7.5 LEFT NE Klickitat St

8.2 LEFT NE 51st Ave

8.3 CHEERS! 3 Bottles (turn around and retrace your way back to **NE Klickitat St** and head east)

8.7 RIGHT NE 57th Ave

9.2 RIGHT NE Sacramento St

9.5 LEFT/CHEERS! NE Sandy Blvd/ 4 Laurelwood Public House and Brewery

9.6 RIGHT/CHEERS! NE 50th Ave/ 5 Gustav's

9.7 LEFT NE Brazee St

10.2 LEFT NE 38th Ave

10.4 RIGHT NE Tillamook St (becomes **NE US Grant Pl**), bicycle route sign to 'Lloyd district'

10.9 LEFT NE 32nd Ave

11.1 RIGHT NE Tillamook St

11.4 LEFT NE 22nd Ave

11.5 RIGHT NE Broadway St

11.9 LEFT NE 15th Ave

12.3 ALERT! After going under overpass, get in far left hand lane to turn at next signal

12.4 LEFT NE 12th Ave

12.8 RIGHT NE Davis St

13.0 LEFT NE 7th Ave

13.1 END/CHEERS! Burnside Brewing

EXTRAS:

6 Grain and Gristle

7 Beaumont Market

8 The Bye and Bye

9 Aviary

10 Community Cycling Center

11 Velo Cult Bike Shop

12 Concordia Ale House

13 Free House

14 Barwares

15 Stanich's

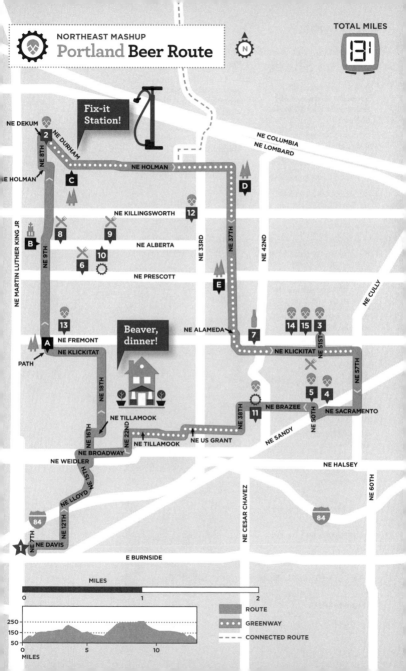

NE EXTENDED ROUTE
Cue Sheet

0.0 START from ⭐ *mile 5.5* of beer route at **NE Holman St and 30th Ave**, head north on NE 30th Ave

0.1 LEFT NE Rosa Parks Way

0.2 RIGHT NE 29th Ave

0.3 RIGHT NE Dekum St

0.5 LEFT/VEER RIGHT NE 33rd Ave/Take exit ramp **ALERT!** Tricky intersection

0.8 VEER RIGHT+ALERT! Merge into far right lane after ramp becomes **NE 33rd Ave**

2.5 LEFT to '**Marine Dr Bike Path**,' unsigned road

2.6 RIGHT to '**Marine Dr Bike Path**' under bridge

3.5 STRAIGHT Cross **Marine Dr** and continue on path

3.9 LOOK! 1 Broughton Beach is on your left

6.7 STRAIGHT Continue on path

7.6 LEFT onto the **Marine Dr** bike lane

8.3 ALERT! Enter bike path again on right side of **Marine Dr**

9.0 ALERT! Path crosses to the other side of **Marine Dr**

10.9 ALERT! Hop back onto **Marine Dr** bike lane

11.9 RIGHT NE Interlachen Ln

13.3 LEFT NE Blue Lake Rd

13.6 LOOK! 2 Blue Lake Regional Park

13.9 LEFT onto the **Marine Dr** bike lane

14.4 LOOK! Reconnect with previous part of route; head back from where you came

18.0 ALERT! Tricky intersection crossing **Marine Dr**

25.4 STRAIGHT NE 33rd Ave goes under overpass bridge

25.6 VEER RIGHT Merge onto **NE Columbia Blvd**

25.7 VEER RIGHT+ALERT! to '**NE 33rd Ave**' up the exit ramp (Careful! Use sidewalk)

26.2 LEFT/END Reconnects with beer route at **NE Holman St** (*mile 5.7*)

Playtime at Broughton Beach.

NE

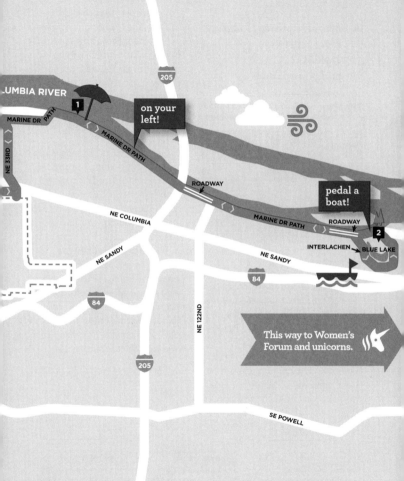

COLUMBIA RIVER

MARINE DR PATH

1

on your left!

MARINE DR PATH

NE 33RD

ROADWAY

NE COLUMBIA

NE SANDY

pedal a boat!

MARINE DR PATH

ROADWAY

2

INTERLACHEN → BLUE LAKE

NE SANDY

84

NE 122ND

84

205

This way to Women's Forum and unicorns.

SE POWELL

MILES
0   1   2   3

ROUTE
GREENWAY
CONNECTED ROUTE

100

0   5   10   15   20   25
MILES

NORTHEAST MASHUP

Ride Stops

▮ Burnside Brewing Company

701 E Burnside St
503-946-8151
burnsidebrewco.com

HOURS: **Mon-Tues 3-10pm, Wed-Fri 3pm-12am, Sat 12pm-12am, Sun 12-10pm**
HAPPY HOUR: **Sun all day, Mon-Fri 3-6pm**

Smack in the middle of a development-plosion that the real estate world likes to call "LoBu" (short for Lower Burnside, a newish zone of hip eating and drinking spots), Burnside Brewing Company goes out of its way to be a different kind of brewpub. Expect to be challenged—not by the atmosphere, unless you find the echo-prone high-ceilinged space too loud—but by the boundary-pushing food and beer. For example, past one-off beers include the Gratzer, a smoked white wheat brew, and the Fruity Monk, a Belgian ale made with fresh pineapple, mango and papaya. If you're feeling less adventurous, the brewery always has its standards on tap, including the Burnside IPA and a reliably delicious stout.

The food runs a strange and adventurous gamut unified by a common ingredient: meat. Think potted braunschweiger with crispy pig ear salad, gnocchi with lamb bolognese, and burgers seared in duck fat. Shared plates, including the housemade sausages, are small. Yes, there are a few items for the non-meat eaters, but meat lovers are the primary audience here. Desserts dabble in molecular gastronomy; play with freeze-dried cookies and powdered sundaes.

PSST!
The budget-minded will love the 20-oz. pints for $3 on Wednesdays.

INSIDER SIP
Try the **Sweet Heat**, a wheat ale made with apricot puree and Scotch Bonnet peppers. Light, fruity and with just enough heat to remind you of last summer's sunburn.

PARK IT
Burnside Brewing slacks a bit on bike parking. There are a couple of bike staples that fill quickly, forcing you to lock to street signs. Upside: plentiful outdoor seating.

NE

2 Breakside Brewery
820 NE Dekum St
503-719-6475
breaksidebrews.com

HOURS: Mon-Thurs 3-10pm, Fri-Sat
12-11pm, Sun 12-10pm | HAPPY HOUR:
Sun-Thurs 3-6pm & 9pm-close

Breakside Brewery is a big, bright hibiscus flower loaded with pollen that attracts cyclists buzzing through the Woodlawn neighborhood. How many breweries offer bike parking covered with a roof garden, plus shiny wooden picnic tables that look like they were designed for parties of 20? While beer geeks may not feel an immediate draw from the bicycle accoutrements, the liquid offerings lure them in.

Breakside makes a range of unique brews that blur the line between food and beer. We're not talking about a "bready" ale or a stout that reminds you of chocolate cream pie, but beer brewed with whole pumpkins, fresh herbs, cedar boughs, chestnuts and lychee. Our taste buds came to attention when we tried the Collaboration Fall

Photo: Scott Lawrence

NE

Harvest Ale, which was brewed with tomatoes, corn, roasted chiles and lime. It tasted like salsa dancing through a New Mexican farmer's market in September. The beer was the first in a long line of collaborative beers, which brewer Ben Edmunds undertakes with local beer bloggers, chefs and bottleshop owners. For example, a delicate fennel farmhouse ale was the brainchild of chef Gabriel Rucker, who owns Portland's beloved Little Bird and Le Pigeon restaurants.

Because it's tucked into the lesser-known residential Woodlawn neighborhood, Breakside can seem off the beaten path (though it is the closest brewery to the airport). We like it that way. More food, we mean beer, for us.

PSST!
The seasonal beers move fast here. If you hear about a good one, don't wait to make a visit.

INSIDER SIP
The **Aztec Ale** is made with cocoa as well as habanero and serrano peppers. Like a spicy Mexican *mole* in a glass, with 9.5% ABV.

PARK IT
Roof garden-covered bike parking next to the spacious outdoor seating.

3 Bottles NW
5015 NE Fremont St
503-287-7022
bottlesnw.com

HOURS: **Mon 4-10pm (no food), Tues-Thurs 3-11pm, Fri-Sat 3pm-12am, Sun 3-10pm** | HAPPY HOUR: **Sun all day, Mon-Fri 3-6pm**

Every neighborhood needs a bottleshop like this, but for those of us who don't call Beaumont or Cully home, it's comforting to know we can visit seven days a week. Bottles is a trifecta of goodness: a beer bar with an insane collection of chilled bottles plus eight rotating taps; a place to hang out, drink and play games; and a barbecue joint.

While the concept sounds schizophrenic, it works. The narrow, low-ceilinged space is divided into distinct zones: a "living room" with a flat-screen TV, a pro blackjack table, a back room with pinball machines and a leafy outdoor beer garden. This is the kind of place where you could clean up at blackjack, tear into ribs at an outdoor picnic table, and sample some interesting beers on tap—all during one action-packed visit.

Beer geeks will enjoy the multiple coolers stocked with an impressive selection of national and international brews, all of which can be opened and enjoyed on-site.

PSST!
Barbecued ribs and pulled pork sell out by 8pm on most nights, after which you're stuck with boxes of Boston Baked Bean candies by the register.

INSIDER SIP
Bartenders here love to talk about the nuances of the beer they serve. Go ahead, geek out.

PARK IT
There are two bike staples conveniently placed out front.

4 Laurelwood Public House & Brewery
5115 NE Sandy Blvd
503-282-0622
laurelwoodbrewpub.com

HOURS: Mon-Wed 11am–10pm, Thurs-Fri 11am–11pm, Sat 10am–11pm, Sun 10am–10pm | HAPPY HOUR: Daily 3-6pm and 9pm-close

Many moons ago, before Lucy had a kid, she went to Laurelwood on a Friday night with her husband. Someone sat them in the dining room where kids were hiding under chairs, dancing on tables and destroying a little play area like Godzillas in Tokyo. All the while, the kids' parents sat at tables, drinking beer as though civilization wasn't collapsing around them. Lucy was appalled. Why hadn't she asked to sit at the bar, where children weren't allowed?

Turns out the brewery is famous for being kid-friendly. But Lucy didn't dismiss Laurelwood, because the beer is that good. Since it opened in 2001, the brewery has established itself as a consistent source of nuanced, balanced beers. Plus, the brewers know how to handle their hops.

The food is standard pub: a sprawling menu of burgers, wraps, nachos and salads that may not satisfy your exotic cravings. Gluten-abstainers will appreciate the GF buns and the kitchen's willingness to customize nearly anything on the menu.

BONUS STOP

Gustav's Bier Stube
5035 NE Sandy Blvd
503-288-5503
gustavs.net/our-beers

HOURS: Sun-Thurs 11am-10pm, Fri-Sat 11am-11pm | HAPPY HOUR: Daily 3-6pm and 9pm-close

When lederhosen-loving Portlanders can't make it to the homeland, they head to one of the city's four **Gustav's**, a bar and shrine to the softer side of German nationalism. You'll find 18 imported German beers on tap and a happy hour menu with potato pancakes topped with lox and horseradish cream, and a molten cheese fondue served with cubes of squishy breads. At the NE location, the bar is attached to **Der Rheinlander** restaurant, where dinner comes with a side of costumed servers singing songs in German to the whine of live accordions.

NE

PSST!
Laurelwood has two locations in the PDX airport past security. That means you can fill a growler for the flight.

INSIDER SIP
Before your eyes glaze over at the thought of another IPA, try the grassy, resinous **Workhorse IPA**, which usually has grapefruit notes.

PARK IT
Around the corner, on NE 51st, is a large bike rack, and there's outdoor seating in back.

NORTHEAST MASHUP

❧ Extras

NIBBLES
Grain and Gristle
473 NE Prescott Ave
503-298-5007
grainandgristle.com

HOURS: Mon-Fri 12pm-12am,
Sat-Sun 9am-3pm and 5-12pm
HAPPY HOUR: Mon-Fri 3-5pm

The Grain and Gristle may not
have the most appetizing name,
but the compact pub fills a com-
monly overlooked niche in the
Rose City by serving both good
food and good beer. We'd call this
place a "gastropub," but the word
seems too pretentious for the
cozy U-shaped space, perfect
for good people-watching.

The owners (including Upright
brewer Alex Ganum; *see page
26*) love beer, and the rotating
taps reveal their expertise for
pairing food and brew. Let the
right pint pique your appetite
for mussels and frites, a soft
pretzel with a zing of mustard,
grilled romaine salad or braised
pork shoulder with baked beans.
Check out the "2-fer" special,
which is always a screaming
deal. Or come for a brunch of
carnitas, beignets or poached
eggs on greens paired with
a pint of farmhouse ale or
Oregon-made cider.

TO GO
Beaumont Market
4130 NE Fremont St
503-284-3032
beaumontmarket.com

HOURS: Daily 7am-10pm

Past the woman pedaling pies
and the pay-by-the-pound frozen
yogurt machine is an unassuming
beer cooler room that will make
you wish you'd brought a sweater
for extended shopping. Some of
Portland's best bottled beers are
featured prominently here, as
are imports from Belgium and
Norway, to name a few.

NE

VEGAN EATS
The Bye and Bye
1011 NE Alberta St
503-281-0537
thebyeandbye.com

HOURS: **Sat-Sun 12pm-12am,
Mon-Thurs 4pm-2am, Fri 2pm-2am**
HAPPY HOUR: **Daily 4-7pm**

Start with the bar's signature drink: a Mason jar filled with peach-infused vodka, peach-infused bourbon, cranberry juice and lemon, which will make you hungry for something from the delicious vegan menu. Consider the weeping tofu sandwich (with a can of PBR) or the spicy "meatball" sandwich. Pro tip: sit within sight of the Evel Knievel portrait. Plenty of bike parking.

PUT A BIRD ON IT
Aviary
1733 NE Alberta St
503-287-2400
aviarypdx.com

HOURS: **Mon-Thur 5-10pm,
Fri-Sat 5-11pm** | HAPPY HOUR:
Mon-Fri 5-7pm

The stark, modern Aviary restaurant is known for its thoughtful wine list and innovative Asian-inspired fare, including the addictive coconut rice with crispy pig ear and Chinese sausage. But don't overlook the bar, a space added after a Fourth of July fire forced renovation. Even though it's an ideal place to enjoy a cocktail bubbling with house-made soda

or one of three beers on tap, the bar isn't an Alberta St destination yet; enjoy the quiet. Combine a few of the happy hour offerings for a perfect meal: kusshi oysters, tempura pumpkin, chicken liver toasts and a hot dog topped with house-made slaw. On "Classy Mondays," slaw dogs and an Old German tall boy are $5 all night long.

NE

ACCESS FOR ALL
Community Cycling Center
1700 NE Alberta St
503-288-8864
communitycyclingcenter.org

HOURS: Mon-Sun 10am-7pm (Mar-Oct),
Mon-Sun 10am-6pm (Nov-Feb)

The Community Cycling Center is unique because it's a non-profit bike shop that does repairs and sells new and used parts and accessories. Their mission is to broaden access to bicycling and its benefits to Portlanders, and their vision is to build a vibrant community where people of all backgrounds use bicycles to stay healthy and connected. Go check it out.

BEERY BIKE SHOP
Velo Cult Bike Shop
1969 NE 42nd Ave
503-922-2012
velocult.com

HOURS: Daily 10am–10pm

Velo Cult is a full-service bike shop that also serves three beers on tap at all times, which can vary from a Pacific Northwest IPA to Pabst. With picnic tables in the middle of the shop and bar stools situated next to the showcased mechanics stands, you can either huddle in a group or gab with the Wrench tweaking your bike as you down a pint.

BEER BRAWL
Concordia Ale House
3276 NE Killingsworth St
503-287-3929
concordia-ale.com

HOURS: Sat-Sun 12pm-12am,
Mon-Thurs 4pm-2am, Fri 2pm-2am
HAPPY HOUR: Daily 4-7pm

We love a good fight, especially if the competition involves drinking beer. Every year, from February to August, Concordia Ale House offers the chance to vote on flights of beer from Oregon, Washington or California. Beers change from week to week, but always feature a few specific styles of beers from one state in each 12-pour flight. You can show up, order the Beer Brawl flight and vote on your favorites. Tallying will always happen after you leave, so be sure to add your name to an email list to find out the results. In the end, one state is declared the ultimate winner.

NE

Fremont Crawl

Take a trip down Fremont St for hip cocktails, road-trip style burgers and more.

Free House
1325 NE Fremont St

HOURS: Daily 4-12pm

With subway tiles, red lighting and serious bartenders in hip wool vests, Free House feels like a friendly little corner of our sister city, Brooklyn. The number of menued cocktails severely dwarfs the beers on hand, so seize the opportunity to have a thoughtful mix of fine bitters and liquors. Highly recommended: the La Paloma #2, a blend of blanco tequila, grapefruit, lime and a few ounces of Rainier Ale. Pairs well with shoestring fries and house-made ketchup, but then again, what doesn't?

Barwares
4605 NE Fremont St
971-229-0995
smallwarespdx.com/ barwares

HOURS: Daily 4pm-2am

Chef Johanna Wares brings a deft touch to memorable food. Her self-proclaimed "inauthentic Asian food," served at both Barwares and the attached Smallwares restaurant, goes well with drink—especially the lemongrass pork sandwich (an elegantly messy bahn mi) and chicken "lollipops" served with Sriracha mayo. Check the "5-for-5" menu, five plates for $5 or less.

Stanich's
4915 NE Fremont St
503-281-2322
stanichs.com

HOURS: Mon-Thurs 11am-10pm, Fri-Sat 11am-11pm

If you adore legendary road trip diners, where Kobe beef and gluten-free buns will never enter the equation, pull over at Stanich's. Since 1949, Stanich's has been making things like the "Special" burger, a grilled beef patty topped with ham, bacon and an egg. Snarf it down among the thick collection of sports pennants, and don't forget to put some quarters in the jukebox before you order.

NE

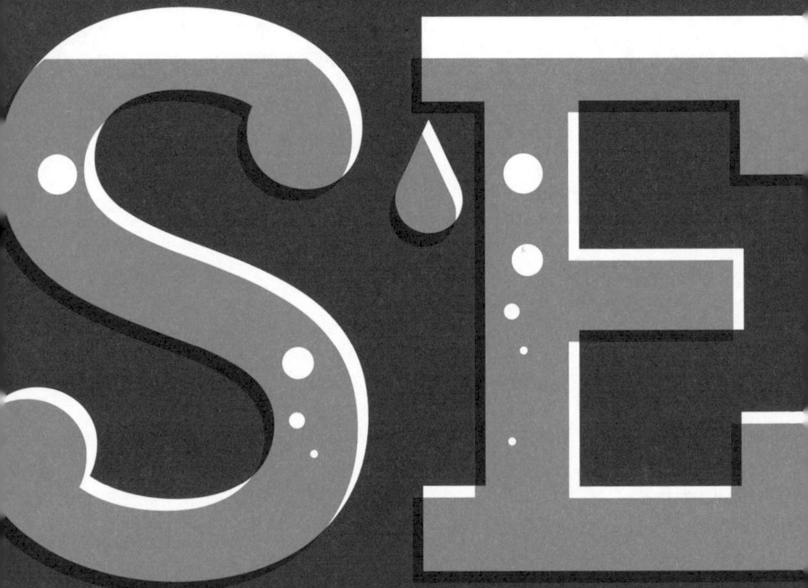
SE

SOUTHEAST BEAST

Sweet Saturation

We're not prone to announcing our favorites. One
movie? One novel? One beer? We plead the fifth.
But we'll boisterously admit that we harbor a deep
love for the Southeast's booming beer scene. Let
the other quadrants weep with envy—the SE is, by far,
the most beer- and bike-saturated
section of town. Somehow the brew
bubble hasn't burst yet. Portland
brewers are constantly eyeing
properties in Southeast and talking
big. Where we see a dilapidated
warehouse, they see the city's
next great barrel-aging facility
and urban hop farm.

The beer and bike scene in the
Southeast is like electrolyte powder
without water, an over-the-top
concentration that can be diluted
to just right. That's why we had
to make some tough decisions:
we simply could not include every single brewery,
bicycle boulevard, brewpub, bike collective, bottleshop
and beer-centric watering hole. Trust us. Your palate
and that lazy bike lock will thank us for sparing you
the ultimate Southeast laundry list.

SPOKES
"The hidden off-road
paths, gravel streets
and back alleys make
Southeast special."

ERIK TONKIN | CO-OWNER
SELLWOOD CYCLE REPAIR
AND CYCLOCROSS CHAMP

SUDS
"Southeast is the
beating heart of the
People's Republic
of Portland. The DIY,
make-your-own-rules
vibe that permeates
this whole city started
here and remains at
the core of everything
we do in Southeast."

VAN HAVIG | BREWER
GIGANTIC BREWING
COMPANY

SE

SOUTHEAST BEAST
Bike Lowdown

BEER ROUTE | 9.4 MILES, MOSTLY EASY

Southeast's love affair with bicycles is less torrid than the newer bicycle love in the other quadrants. This hood's affinity for bikes is long-term monogamous and has role-modeled alternative transportation for the rest of the city. Don't get us wrong: there's still spice in this relationship. Don't be surprised if you see a leopard-print tall bike or folks hauling a couch via bamboo trailer.

The ride starts at **Hair of the Dog Brewing**, which happens to be at the base of the city's new bicycle/pedestrian addition to the **Morrison Bridge**. Excellent bike watching.

The route goes past bike art enhancements on signs and streets (such as on **SE Clinton St**, *mile 2*), bike corrals, sharrows, green boxes and bicycle boulevards, all of which create a healthy sampling of the infrastructure that makes Portland a rock star bike city.

Take note that **SE Clinton St** (*mile 2*) and **SE Ankeny St** (*mile 6.7*) are happening bike boulevards with busy eateries, bustling coffee shops with outdoor seating, and boutique bike shops.

You'll pass **Laurelhurst Park** (*mile 6.9*), a succulent green oasis smack dab in the middle of busy streets and a fancy urban neighborhood. Laurelhurst's landscaping was designed by the firm of famous architect **Frederick Law Olmsted**, who co-designed Central Park in New York City. It's the perfect place to have a picnic break in the middle of your tour de beer.

SE LADD'S ADDITION
In the early 1900s, the labyrinthine diagonal streets of **Ladd's Addition** (*mile 1.3*) were a radical departure from the standard neighborhood grid. More artistic than utilitarian, Ladd's has four diamond-shaped rose gardens at the four compass points and a central circle with a communal landscaped lawn. Ladd's is best by bike: rose-scented, low-traffic and fanciful.

KEGS BY BIKE
Hopworks Urban Brewery (*page 27*) owner **Christian Ettinger** and cargo bike makers at **Metrofiets** (*metrofiets.com*) put their heads together to create Portland's 10-foot-long beer bike, replete with two keg-holders and bar counter.

SE

EXTENDED BIKE NERD ROUTE | 13.4 MILES, MODERATE | 960 FT GAIN

Portland cyclists love to swirl their way to the top of Mt Tabor and Rocky Butte, two easily accessible dormant volcanoes. Both mini-peaks, incidentally, offer expansive big-daddy volcano vistas and a nature fix for the urbanite.

Volcano Love

RIDE GIST
Two medium-sized climbs don't deter many cyclists from making this a quick post-work ride. **Moderate**.

PULL OVER
Pie at the **Bipartisan Cafe** (*mile 3.8*).

BEST VIEW
Tie between the top of **Mt Tabor** and **Rocky Butte**.

Bulging in the middle of flattish Southeast, **Mt Tabor** reigns over the neighborhood. Unlike jagged, snow-topped **Mt Hood** and **Mt St. Helens**, which you can see from its summit, **Mt Tabor** (*mile 0.5*) is a landscaped princess who unfolds the green carpet for picnickers, power-walking grandmothers and ecstatic dogs romping in circles around flirting masters. Cyclists take advantage of Tabor's forest trails and paved paths snaking through the 195 wooded acres.

Rocky Butte, a cinder cone butte, is crowned with **Joseph Wood Hill Park** (*mile 7.7*), which has an expansive view of the snow-capped volcanoes and the bustling valley. It's the perfect place to smooch your honey or stop for a bite to eat.

On the loop back to the Southeast beer trail, you cycle **NE Tillamook St** (*mile 10.8*), a popular bike boulevard.

SE

STOP IN
Check out these cool velo retailers on the beer route: employee-owned **City Bikes Coop** (*mile 8.1, citybikes. coop*) and **Splendid Cycles** (*mile 0.8, splendidcycles.com*), a cargo bike boutique.

SE HAWTHORNE BIKE BROWSING
The Hawthorne District is home to eclectic shops we love: **Coventry** (*coventrycycle.com*, 2025 SE Hawthorne Blvd), a recumbent oasis; **Bikeasaurus** (*bikeasaurus.com*, 1725 SE Hawthorne Blvd), a gift shop dedicated to bike culture; and **Clever Cycles** (*clevercycles.com*, 900 SE Hawthorne Blvd), which specializes in family bicycle transportation.

SE BEER ROUTE
Cue Sheet

0.0 START from ⭐ **Hair of the Dog Brewing**, head south on **SE Water St**

0.1 LEFT SE Taylor St

0.3 LEFT SE 7th Ave

0.4 RIGHT SE Belmont St

0.5 CHEERS! 2 Cascade Brewing Barrel House/ 19 Green Dragon Bistro

0.8 BIKES! 20 Splendid Cycles

0.9 RIGHT SE 16th Ave

1.2 STRAIGHT SE 16th Ave jogs to the left crossing **SE Hawthorne Blvd**. Use cross walk if there's traffic.

1.3 LEFT/RIGHT SE Maple Ave/SE Poplar Ave

1.5 RIGHT Take the round-about, **SE Ladd Ave**

1.6 RIGHT Exit roundabout on **SE Elliot Ave**

1.8 CHEERS! Walk your bike across **SE Division St** to 3 **Apex**

1.9 LEFT onto **SE 11th Ave** from Apex

2.0 LEFT SE Clinton St (Keep an eye out for bike art)

OPTIONAL SIDE TRIP: ▶
2.5 CHEERS! Take **SE 21st Ave** to go to **7 Gigantic Brewing**

3.7 LEFT SE 41st Ave

4.3 CHEERS! 11 Hawthorne Hophouse

4.4 RIGHT SE Salmon St

4.6 LEFT/RIGHT SE 46th Ave/SE Salmon St

4.8 LEFT/RIGHT SE 49th Ave/SE Taylor St

5.2 LEFT/RIGHT SE 55th Ave/SE Yamhill St

5.4 LEFT/RIGHT SE 60th Ave/SE Belmont St

5.5 CHEERS! 13 Cheese Bar/head west on **SE Belmont St** *For less traffic, use SE Salmon St to 45th then head north to hook back up with the route at SE Belmont.*

6.2 CHEERS!/RIGHT 12 Horse Brass Pub/ SE 45th Ave

6.4 CHEERS!/LEFT 14 Belmont Station/ **SE Stark St**

6.4 RIGHT/LEFT SE 44th Ave/SE Oak Ct

6.5 RIGHT SE 41st Ave

6.7 LEFT SE Ankeny St

6.9 LOOK! Get off bike and use cross walk over **SE 39th Ave** if traffic is bad; A **Laurelhurst Park**

7.6 CHEERS! 4 Coalition Brewing

8.1 BIKES! 18 City Bikes Coop

8.5 LEFT SE Sandy Blvd, becomes **SE 7th Ave**

9.1 RIGHT SE Taylor St

9.4 RIGHT SE Water St

9.4 END/CHEERS! ⭐ Hair of the Dog Brewing

Bike art on SE Clinton St.

EXTRAS:
5 **Harvester Brewing**
6 **Bushwacker Cider**
7 **Gigantic Brewing**
8 **Bar Avignon**
9 **Victory Bar**
10 **Inn Beervana**
11 **Hawthorne Hophouse**
12 **Horse Brass Pub**
13 **Cheese Bar**
14 **Belmont Station**
15 **Coventry Cycle**
16 **Bikeasaurus**
17 **Clever Cycles**

ROUTE
GREENWAY
CONNECTED ROUTE
OPTIONAL SIDE TRIP

SE

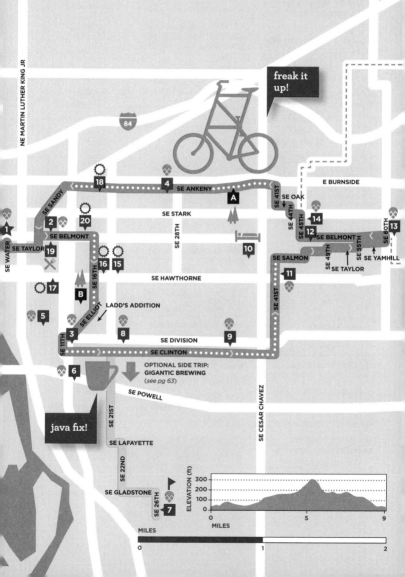

SE EXTENDED ROUTE
Cue Sheet

0.0 RIGHT/LEFT heading west from 🧀 **Cheese Bar** on **SE Belmont St/SE 60th Ave** (traffic)

0.2 LEFT SW Salmon St, to 'Mt Tabor Park'

0.5 LEFT Hard turn before the reservoir

0.9 RIGHT at stop sign, heading towards playground

1.0 VEER RIGHT at V, going up past white gate

1.3 VEER RIGHT at V, when you get to the loop at the top/**A Mt Tabor**

1.6 ALERT! Go back down from where you came

1.9 RIGHT Hard turn past white gate

2.1 VEER RIGHT at unmarked intersection

2.5 LEFT Hard turn past gates

2.9 LEFT SE 76th Ave

3.6 RIGHT SE Washington St

3.7 LEFT/LEFT SE 78th Ave/SE Stark St (**2 Bipartisan Cafe** ½ a block east on SE Stark)

3.8 RIGHT SE 76th Ave

4.0 LEFT E Burnside St

4.1 RIGHT NE 74th Ave

4.9 LEFT/RIGHT NE Halsey St/NE 74th Ave, following 'Bike Route'

5.2 RIGHT NE Tillamook St

5.9 LEFT NE 88th Ave

6.1 RIGHT NE Russell St

6.3 VEER RIGHT/LEFT NE 92nd Ave/NE Rocky Butte Rd

6.7 ALERT! Short tunnel

7.6 RIGHT/LEFT at T near castle-like structure/on gravel road blocked off to cars

7.7 LOOK! Take small loop around top of **B Rocky Butte** and go back down gravel road

7.8 STRAIGHT as you leave gravel road, continue on unsigned road directly ahead

9.2 RIGHT/LEFT NE Hill Way/NE 89th Ave

9.3 RIGHT NE Siskiyou St

9.4 RIGHT/LEFT NE Fremont Dr/NE Siskiyou St

9.9 LEFT NE 77th Ave, becomes **SE Sacramento St**

10.4 LEFT NE 72nd Dr, hard turn

10.8 RIGHT NE Tillamook St

11.3 LEFT NE 62nd Ave

11.4 RIGHT NE Hancock St

11.8 LEFT NE 53rd Ave

12.6 RIGHT NE Everett St

12.9 LEFT/RIGHT NE 47th Ave/NE Davis St

13.0 LEFT NE 45th Ave

13.4 END Reconnects with beer route at **SE Stark St** (*mile 6.4*)

Rocky Butte views.

SE

SE POWELL

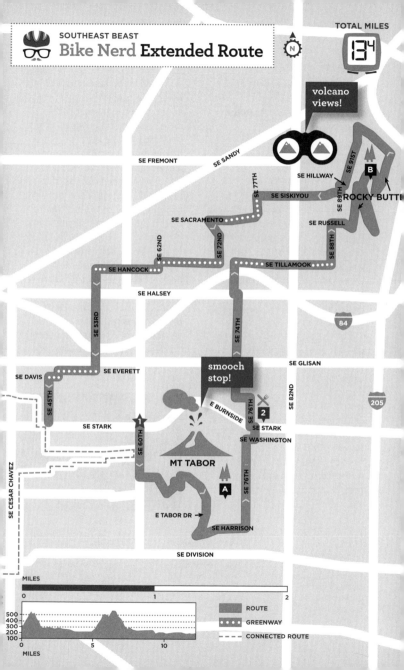

SOUTHEAST BEAST

Ride Stops

1 Hair of the Dog Brewing
61 SE Yamhill St
503-232-6585
hairofthedog.com

HOURS: **Wed-Thurs 2-8pm, Fri-Sat 11:30am-10pm, Sun 11:30am-8pm**

It's easy to feel small inside this big, boxy former warehouse. Plenty of details help create scale, including bright turquoise walls, a wood bar and street-level view of the downtown skyline. But what really looms large here are Hair of the Dog's outstanding ales.

For many years, owner and brewer Alan Sprints threw an annual "dock sale" where he sold cases of new and vintage brews. Super fans would line up in the wee hours of the morning and drink beer (duh), as they waited to snatch up $200 cases, like bargain hunters at Walmart before Black Friday (only with fewer tramplings and more giddy happiness).

Those dock sales ended when the brewery moved to its current location, but the fanaticism for the beer did not. The crux of the cult following lies in the fact that these beers were made to be cellared and aged, which makes them highly collectible. The complex, big beers are named after Sprints' friends and craft beer pioneers: Fred, Adam, Ruth, Matt, Michael. In the tasting room, you can order rare bottles, such as some "From the Wood" beers, but you must drink them on-site (the brewery's attempt to put the smackdown on eBay hawkers). Take your time no matter what you drink. These beers deserve your full attention.

PSST!
Owner/brewer **Alan Sprints** likes to cook. The menu, which includes short ribs braised in beer and mac & cheese, is his doing.

INSIDER SIP
Blue Dot is one of the more delicate and interesting IPAs in town.

PARK IT
There are a number of bike staples, plus outdoor seating where you can easily sit next to and/or watch your bike.

SE

2 Cascade Brewing Barrel House

939 SE Belmont St

503-265-8603

cascadebrewing barrelhouse.com

HOURS: Sun-Mon 12-10pm, Tues-Thurs 12-11pm, Fri-Sat 12pm-12am

Like the world's biggest ball of twine, Cascade Brewing Barrel House is an oddity you won't soon forget. After all, how often do you get to hang out in a building filled with big oak barrels bubbling with beers-in-progress? Unlike that ball of twine, however, you'll want to visit the Barrel House again and again.

That's because the beers here are barrel-aged sour ales, blended with everything from figs and peaches to lemon peel to apricots. And they rotate frequently, so you can try, say, a sour blonde ale aged in oak for eight months then finished with fresh lime zest. Or the Sang Noir, a double red aged in whiskey and port barrels then blended with cherries.

The Barrel House is the offspring of Cascade Brewing's Raccoon Lodge, a brewery in the outskirts of Portland. All the beer is brewed at the mother ship before it's aged and blended at the Barrel House. Some barrels are even tapped right behind the bar. Pucker up, buttercup.

BONUS STOP
The Green Dragon Bistro and Brewpub

928 SE 9th Ave

503-517-0660

pdxgreendragon.com

HOURS: Sun-Wed 11am-11pm, Thurs-Sat 11-1am | HAPPY HOUR: Daily 4-6pm, Thurs-Sat 10pm-close, Sun-Wed 9pm-close

With more than 50 beers on tap, **The Green Dragon** is for people who relish the chance to stew in indecision. "The Dragon" has become an important gathering place for beer geeks, thanks to the vast selection, alluringly dark warehouse space and close-in location. The bar is owned by **Rogue Brewing**, which has other locations in town (see Northwest, *page 93*), but the beer brewed on-site is released under the **Buckman Brewery** label. Some of the herbal, non-hopped Buckman beers are on tap here. Pro tip: Wear a Hawaiian shirt on Tuesdays and your second pint is free.

SE

PSST!
This is no fancy wine bar. Sports are on the TV behind the bar, and food is served in plastic baskets.

INSIDER SIP
Every Tuesday at 6pm, a guest taps the barrel of the day, which often includes a spray of beer that the Barrel House likes to call a "sour shower."

PARK IT
Sadly, there are only a couple of bike staples around the corner, but the wrought metal fence around the outdoor seating will do.

3 Apex
1216 SE Division St
503-273-9227
apexbar.com

HOURS: **Daily 11:30-2:30am**

Cyclists and bikers (as in motorcycles) receive primo treatment here, with plenty of parking for both inside the picnic-table-packed beer garden. Car drivers, on the other hand, must fend for themselves on trafficky SE Division St.

After basking in the two-wheeled love outside, head indoors to peruse the 50 (!) beers on tap. A computerized screen behind the bar keeps the tap listings fresh, and a few tables, barstools and some sweet pinball machines make the bar area a happy hangout on rainy days. But, in all honesty, we'd rather be in the beer garden, barring snow or torrents of rain. As you might imagine, the beer list has something for every mood, occasion and thirst, but don't show up hungry. There's no food on-site, but you're welcome to bring your own eats, like our favorite—a killer bahn mi from Double Dragon across the street.

SE

PSST!
The "no" list: dogs, kids and credit cards. The "yes" list: beer, pinball and food from elsewhere.

INSIDER SIP
Unlike most online tap listings, Apex's lineup is always up to date, as it matches the list behind the bar:
apexbar.com/menu

PARK IT
Unparalleled bike parking in the streetside beer garden. Use a lock if you plan to spend time indoors.

4 Coalition Brewing Co.
2724 SE Ankeny St
503-894-8080
coalitionbrewing.com

HOURS: **Tues-Fri 3pm-12am, Sat-Sun 12pm-12am** | HAPPY HOUR: **Tues-Sun 3-6pm**

We have a soft spot for pubs that seem like they're rosy-cheeked cousins of Powell's Books, places where you can quietly sit with a book and a pint and while away a rainy afternoon. Coalition fits the bill. On less bookish days, when the sun is out, sidewalk picnic tables beckon swillers who don't mind dogs padding by with their owners.

The solid rotation of balanced beers are brewed right across the street in a former call center. Special one-offs and seasonals are also worth trying, but the best ones go fast. For example, you may need to work some social-media magic to figure out if that one-off smoky Dunkel still exists.

In a nod to DIYers, the brewery offers the "Coalator Program," which allows talented home brewers to make their recipes in the brewery then serve their beers in the pub, alongside big-boy Coalition beers. Ask the bartender if a Coalator is on tap and help reward all those sweaty hours spent boiling wort (the beer before it becomes beer) in home kitchens.

SE

PSST!
The food is made by a former food cart called **Savvy J's**, which went brick-and-mortar when they partnered with Coalition.

INSIDER SIP
There's no better deal than the $2.50 pints on Wednesdays and $10 pitchers on Sundays.

PARK IT
Around the corner from Coalition is one of Portland's famous bike corrals equipped with tons of staples.

SOUTHEAST BEAST

✿ Extras

NIBBLES

Cheese Bar
6031 SE Belmont St
503-222-6014
cheese-bar.com

HOURS: Tues-Sun 11am-11pm

Oenophiles love to claim cheese as their thing, but let's get real, wine usually brings too much acidity to the party. Cheese belongs with beer. Just ask cheesemonger and Cheese Bar owner Steve Jones, who intimately understands how beer and cheese nudge each other toward transcendence. Stuff your ego in the pannier when you walk into Cheese Bar; it's okay if you haven't yet tasted every cheese sitting snugly inside the glass case. Let the staff help you create some perfect pairings: a board of stinky cheeses with a barrel-aged sour or a French wheat beer with a manchego (just don't tell the Spanish).

TO GO

Belmont Station
4500 SE Stark St
503-232-8538
belmont-station.com

HOURS: Bottleshop: Mon-Sat 10am-10pm, Sun 12-10pm, Biercafé: Mon-Thurs 2-11pm, Fri-Sun 12-11pm

Take a trip around the globe at Belmont Station, Portland's premier bottleshop and a hub of the city's beer scene. Many of Portland's best brewers, beer bloggers and other industry folks worked at Belmont Station at one point in their careers. The Belmont Station staff know their stuff and will happily educate about the 1,200 beers in stock. Even though you might be here to buy a bottle for the road, don't overlook the attached Biercafé, where the 16 beers on tap are always interesting and sometimes rare.

SE

NEW BREWS

Gigantic Brewing Company Tap Room and Champagne Lounge
5224 SE 26th Ave
503-208-3416
giganticbrewing.com

HOURS: Mon-Fri 3-9pm, Sat 2-9pm, Sun 2-8pm

Situated in a warehouse district close to Reed College, this recent addition to Portland's brewery scene features a short list of one-offs, plus a year-round IPA. Guest taps include some of the best from the Northwest. As a beer bar oddity, the "champagne" list makes carbonation the common currency. But none of the sparkling wines are served by the glass, so be ready to commit to a bottle. Great bike parking and outdoor seating, plus the ubiquitous roll-up doors. No food available on-site; pizza deliveries recommended.

STAY AWHILE

Inn Beervana
Corner of SE 38th Ave and SE Main St
503-232-8538
beerodyssey.com/RWB/ InnBeervana.htm

RATES: $140/night (2 night min)

Only in Portland will you find Inn Beervana, a beer-themed B&B (you'll sleep under a hop mural, naturally) that's perfectly situated for beersplorations by bike. Proprietors Kimberley and Brian Yaeger welcome guests to their slice of hop heaven with a six-pack of Oregon beer in the mini-fridge and free advice about experiencing Beervana. Cyclists can take advantage of covered parking under an outdoor lean-to.

SE

Photo: Lara Ferroni

GLUTEN-FREE BEER

Harvester Brewing
715 SE Lincoln Street
503-928-4195
harvesterbrewing.com

HOURS: **Thurs 3:30-6pm**

Harvester Brewing is the only dedicated gluten-free brewery in the country. The beers are made with as many Oregon ingredients as possible: chestnuts, sorghum, gluten-free oats and Willamette Valley hops. There are limited tasting room hours, but you can find these beers at a variety of restaurants, stores and bottleshops in Oregon and Washington.

OTHER SIPS

Bushwhacker Cider
1212 D SE Powell Blvd
503-445-0577
bushwhackercider.com

HOURS: **Mon 5-11pm, Tues-Thurs 2-11pm, Fri-Sat 12pm-12am, Sun 12-11pm**

Welcome to the delicious world of hard ciders at Bushwacker, a "cider bar" that serves dozens of types of the bubbly beverage on tap and in bottles. Try the five-pour flight for $5, which may include one of Bushwhacker's house creations, such as a non-carbonated version aged in gin barrels.

SE

Raising the Bar

These Southeast bars are some of our favorite places to grab a drink.

Horse Brass Pub
4534 SE Belmont Street
503-232-2202
horsebrass.com

HOURS: **Daily 11-2:30am**

We'd like to designate the Horse Brass as the best place to eat a Scotch egg. It's a broody English-styled bar that makes you want to spill your secrets to the stranger next to you or eat some fish and chips. More importantly, you'll want to order a craft beer from the solid list. The bar has been a pivotal part of the city's beer scene since 1976, thanks to founder and owner Don Younger, a important character in Portland's beer world. Sadly, Don passed away in 2011, but his spirit lives on inside the Horse Brass with every unapologetic pint.

The Victory Bar
3652 SE Division St
503-236-8755
thevictorybar.com

HOURS: **Mon-Sat 5pm-1am, Sun 5pm-12am**
HAPPY HOUR: **Daily 5-7pm, 11pm-12am**

This bar oozes hipster cool, but in a way that prioritizes rare Belgian wheat beers over PBR. Six rotating taps and a globe-trotting bottle list, which includes some cellared gems, make the unforgettable venison burger and Gruyere spaetzel more like opening acts to the beery headliners.

Bar Avignon
2138 SE Division St
503-517-0808
baravignon.com

HOURS: **Daily 5pm-close**
HAPPY HOUR: **Mon-Fri 5-6pm**

Bar Avignon whisks us off our feet and makes us swoon. What puts the accent over our "é"? The sweet cafe sidewalk tables, oysters on the half shell, crispy duck fat potatoes and pretty much anything that comes out of the

kitchen. A giant wall of wine leads some to call this place a "wine bar," but with seven serious Pacific Northwest taps and a list of perfect cocktails, we prefer "dream bar." Order a glass of rosé or a pastis. We won't tell your brew crew.

Hawthorne Hophouse
4111 SE Hawthorne Blvd
503-477-9619
oregonhophouse.com

HOURS: **Sun-Thurs 12pm-12am, Fri-Sat 12pm-2am** | HAPPY HOUR: **Sun all day, Mon-Sat 3-6pm & 9pm-12am**

The *Cheers* theme song could be playing as you walk into this neighborhood haunt. If you can't decide on one of the 24 Northwest beers on tap, the server can point you towards an IPA that won't wallop you with hops or a stout that drinks like breakfast. The typical crowd: cyclists, hipsters, fleeced-out office workers and couples on first dates. Live music on some evenings may induce free-form interpretive dance (hey, there's a head shop next door), but don't count on intimate conversation during the show.

SE

SOUTHWEST UNDRESSED

Suits, Ties and Barflies

Downtown, the heart of this quadrant, buzzes during business hours, but the beer scene is quieter than in other quadrants. Cycle-commuting professionals flood in and out of Southwest every day because a bicycle is the fastest, easiest way to get around. Besides commuters, bike messengers zip around this zone, and cargo bike couriers deliver soup and pizza.

Most large-scale brewing happens in the outskirts of this quadrant, but there are some classic, don't-miss beer spots downtown, such as a tiny literary-tinged brewery and a bright and airy taproom with some of the finest beers in any part of town. Plus, there's a historic bar owned by one of the city's bike-loving former mayors. No matter where you choose to go, trade the forehead vein-popping experience of driving a car downtown for a bike ride.

SPOKES

"The West Hills bring the pain, but the volcano views from Council Crest answer with glory."

CHRIS DIMINNO | CHEF AND TRAIL SHREDDER CLYDE COMMON

SUDS

"The ultimate Portland commute begins with great hills and ends with killer brews."

GREG HIGGINS | CHEF AND OWNER | HIGGINS RESTAURANT

SW

SOUTHWEST UNDRESSED
Bike Lowdown

BEER ROUTE | 3.6 MILES, EASY

The short-but-sweet Southwest beer route tours iconic Portland places, like the staging zone for the Saturday Market, the fountains and crowds of the Waterfront Esplanade, and newer spots like Carfree Ankeny. But you'll have to keep your cycling wits about you due to traffic (*see below*) in Portland's pulsing business district, where movers and shakers have places to be.

The bike lane on **SW Jefferson St** (*mile 0.1*) is one of the best ways to head west, and the bike lane on **SW Broadway Ave** (*mile 1.8*) for heading south. Recently, an extra-roomy bike lane appeared on **SW Stark St** (*mile 1.5*). It would be king of downtown bike infrastructure except the lane is so spacious that cars illegally use it.

Watch out coming down **SW Salmon St** from **SW 20th Ave** (*mile 0.8*). It is steep and can be trafficky.

At *mile 2.3,* you'll pass the staging area for the **Saturday Market**, an iconic Portland weekend event that happens March through December. Music, artisans, tourists, locals and food vendors all meld together.

On a sparkling summer day, the broad Southwest **Waterfront Esplanade** (*mile 2.5*) bubbles over with roller-bladers, cyclists, runners, families, lovers and street kids. You won't go fast, but this section always makes us think, "We love this town."

Where **SW Ankeny St** (*mile 2.4*) and **Salmon St** (*mile 3*) intersect at the **Waterfront Esplanade**, you'll be tempted to splash around public fountains with the euphoric kiddos. We were.

HEADS UP DOWNTOWN
Traffic is dense and requires awareness and metro bicycle skills, especially during rush hours. FYI, you can get a citation for riding on the sidewalk. Traffic moves at about 15 mph, so take the whole lane. It's legal. P.S. Watch out for MAX tracks (*pg 83*).

CARFREE ANKENY
In 2011, the city and business owners grumbled about an experimental pilot program that closed the little alley of **SW Ankeny St** (*mile 2.2*) between 2nd and 3rd Ave to cars. However, pedestrians and cyclists came in droves to the outdoor picnic tables, and businesses thrived. Carfree Ankeny has been indefinitely extended.

SW

▶
ADD 180 FT GAIN
FOR COUNCIL CREST
SIDE TRIP OPTION

EXTENDED BIKE NERD ROUTE | 18.5 MILES, DIFFICULT | 2500 FT GAIN

In full disclosure, this is one of our regular rides. While researching it for you, we realized how lucky we are to be able to saunter out our front doors and cycle this route. It supremely rocks—from the fabulous Southeast Waterfront Esplanade and quiet roads through a historic cemetery to one of the best views in the city.

Best of the West

RIDE GIST
Bring your hardy climbing game for the 2,680 ft of elevation gain. **Difficult**.

PULL OVER
Smell the roses, literally, at the famous **Washington Park International Rose Test Garden**.

BEST VIEW
Council Crest (*mile 13.3*), PDX's highest point, has volcanoes in every direction.

Head south on the **Springwater Corridor**. Highlights include river views, **Oaks Bottom Wildlife Refuge** (*mile 2.6*) and all species of PDX cyclists.

In **River View Cemetery** (*mile 4.7*), roads wind past incredible landscaping and crumbling mausoleums. There are more views of **Mt Hood** than cars.

On **SW Westwood Dr** (*mile 8.8*), the unmaintained, chewed-up pavement climbs steeply. You can do it!

The **Fairmount Loop** (*mile 10.6*) swoops next to **Marquam Nature Park**. There are no sidewalks; watch out for pedestrians!

From **Council Crest** (*turnoff at mile 12.6*), Portland's highest point, see five Cascade peaks. Stand in the middle of the circle on top and sing. You'll see.

SW Skyline Blvd (*mile 14.1*) has spots with no shoulder.

The descent through **Forest Park** (*mile 15.5*) is killer, past the **Oregon Zoo** (*mile 15.8*) and **Washington Park International Rose Test Garden** (*mile 17.3*).

MESSENGER MECCA
Bike messengers hang at **Stumptown Coffee** (*stumptowncoffee. com*, 128 SW 3rd Ave) or swill cheap happy hour beer at **XV** (15 SW 2nd Ave). This tattooed brand of notorious, attitude-slinging cyclist—equipped with ironic mullets, double-take piercings and one defiant gear—are less prevalent these days. See 'em while you can! They are so cute and angsty.

Upright and cheery cargo-bike delivery services, like **Portland Pedal Power** (*portland pedalpower.com*), are encroaching on the messenger gig.

SW

SW BEER ROUTE
Cue Sheet

0.0 START From ⭐ **Higgins Restaurant**, head west on **SW Jefferson St**

0.6 CHEERS! 2 **Goose Hollow Pub**

0.7 RIGHT SW 20th Ave

0.8 RIGHT SW Salmon St (watch for traffic)

1.1 LEFT SW 14th Ave (quick transfer to left lane)

1.3 RIGHT SW Alder St

1.4 LEFT SW 12th Ave (quick transfer to left lane)

1.5 RIGHT SW Stark St

1.6 CHEERS! 5 **Clyde Common**

1.7 LEFT/RIGHT/CHEERS! SW Park Ave/SW Ankeny St/ 5 **Tugboat Brewing**

1.8 CHEERS!/RIGHT 3 **Bailey's Taproom/SW Broadway Ave**

1.9 LEFT SW Stark St

2.1 LEFT SW 4th Ave

2.2 RIGHT/LOOK! SW Ankeny St (just past street with 'Do Not Enter' sign)/ Walk your bike on A **Carfree Ankeny** between SW 3rd and 2nd. B **Saturday Market** straight ahead.

2.5 RIGHT on C **Waterfront Esplanade** multi-use path

3.0 RIGHT/LEFT after D **SW Salmon St Fountain**, follow bike route sign to 'Downtown'/on multi-use path to 'Westbound Traffic,' and head west off the Hawthorne Bridge.

3.2 LEFT SW 1st Ave

3.3 RIGHT SW Jefferson St

3.6 END/CHEERS! ⭐ **Higgins Restaurant**

EXTRAS:

A **Carfree Ankeny**

B **Saturday Market**

C **Waterfront Esplanade**

D **Salmon St Fountain**

4 **Tugboat Brewing**

5 **Clyde Common**

A springtime view of the Waterfront Esplanade (NW) from the Hawthorne Bridge.

Photo: Leah Nash

Bike messengers caffeinating between deliveries.

SW

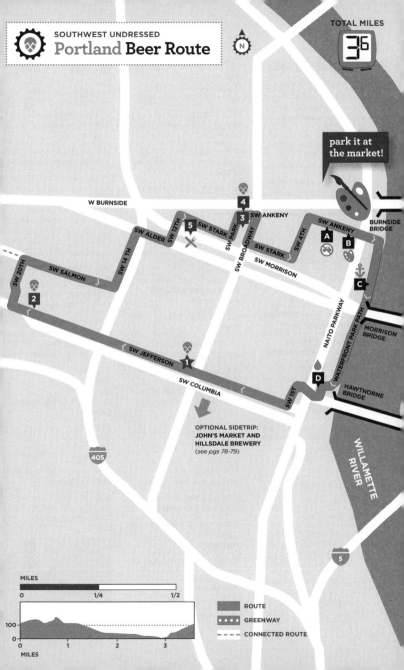

SOUTHWEST UNDRESSED
Portland Beer Route

N

TOTAL MILES
3.6

park it at
the market!

W BURNSIDE

SW ANKENY

SW STARK

SW ALDER

SW SALMON

SW JEFFERSON

SW COLUMBIA

OPTIONAL SIDETRIP:
JOHN'S MARKET AND
HILLSDALE BREWERY
(see pgs 78-79)

BURNSIDE
BRIDGE

MORRISON
BRIDGE

HAWTHORNE
BRIDGE

WILLAMETTE
RIVER

NAITO PARKWAY

WATERFRONT PARK PATH

SW 20TH

SW 14TH

SW 12TH

SW PARK

SW BROADWAY

SW 4TH

SW 1ST

SW MORRISON

405

5

MILES

0   1/4   1/2

100

0   1   2   3

MILES

ROUTE

GREENWAY

CONNECTED ROUTE

SW EXTENDED ROUTE
Cue Sheet

0.0 START ⭐ Go straight instead of right at *mile 3* of the beer route, going under the **Hawthorne Bridge**

0.1 RIGHT at bike path route to 'SE Portland,' accessing Hawthorne Bridge

0.5 RIGHT/LEFT Follow bike path route sign to 'Eastbank Esplanade'/onto **Eastbank Esplanade**

1.0 LEFT at Springwater Corridor map, following signs to the 'Springwater Corridor Trail'

1.1 RIGHT Following the bike route sign to 'Springwater Corridor Trail'

1.2 LOOK! Enter **Springwater Corridor Trail.**

2.6 LOOK! **Oaks Bottom Wildlife Refuge.**

4.2 LEFT/RIGHT at stop sign, follow bike route sign to 'Sellwood Bridge'/SE Grand Ave, past Dead End sign, to 'Sellwood Bridge'

4.3 RIGHT+ALERT! Cross over the **Sellwood Bridge** on sidewalk. Warning: narrow sidewalk. Walk bike for safety.

4.6 VEER RIGHT From sidewalk, enter road and take the exit to '**43 South, Lake Oswego**'

4.7 STRAIGHT at stop light, into the **B Riverview Cemetery** and follow main road and bike markers

5.3 LEFT/LEFT Hard turn following bike marker/to 'Chapel' following bike marker

5.5 LEFT Following bike marker, not to 'Chapel'

5.6 RIGHT/LEFT Following bike marker/ Hard turn following bike marker

5.7 RIGHT following bike marker

5.9 STRAIGHT at 4-way intersection, following bike marker

6.1 VEER RIGHT following bike marker

6.2 LEFT following bike marker

6.4 RIGHT leaving cemetery, unsigned **SW Palatine Hill Rd**

6.7 RIGHT/LEFT SW Boones Ferry Rd/SW Primrose St

6.8 RIGHT SW Terwilliger Blvd

7.7 STRAIGHT through SW Barbur Blvd intersection

8.8 LEFT SW Westwood Dr, following bike route sign to '**Multnomah Village**' *Rough road till mile 10.6*
OR
STRAIGHT to cut out much climbing and head straight back to downtown

9.3 RIGHT at stop sign continuing on **SW Westwood Dr**

9.6 LEFT SW Menefee Dr, turns into **SW Westwood Dr**

9.8 RIGHT SW Westwood View, becomes **SW Mitchell St**

10.0 LEFT SW Mitchell St

10.6 RIGHT SW Fairmount Blvd

12.4 LEFT SW Talbot Rd (turn sneaks up on you)

12.6 STRAIGHT at stop sign, continuing on **SW Talbot Rd**
OR
OPTIONAL SIDETRIP: ▶ **C LEFT** Hard turn, **Council Crest** option (*adds 1.5 miles and 180 ft of climbing*)

12.7 STRAIGHT at stop light onto **SW Humphrey Blvd**

14.1 RIGHT/RIGHT+ALERT! on easy to miss turn onto ped/bike sidewalk connecting SW Humphrey Blvd to **SW Skyline Blvd**/ SW Skyline Blvd (*Caution getting into the bike lane on this busy road.*)

14.9 RIGHT SW Fairview Blvd

15.5 RIGHT SW Knights Blvd, to '**Washington Park**'

15.8 LEFT/LOOK!+ALERT! SW Kingston Dr, to 'Rose Garden'. **D** 'Zoo' to right. *Watch out for potholes!*

17.3 RIGHT SW Sherwood Blvd
OR
STRAIGHT to **E** 'Rose Garden'

18.0 RIGHT at Reservoir, to 'City Center'

18.2 RIGHT SW Park Pl

18.4 RIGHT/LEFT SW King Ave/SW Salmon St

18.5 END Reconnects with beer route at **SW 20th Ave** and **SW Salmon St** (*mile .8*)

Summiting Council Crest.

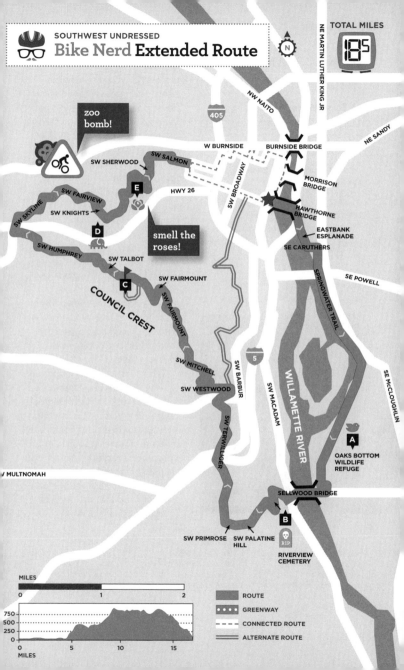

SOUTHWEST UNDRESSED

Ride Stops

1 Higgins restaurant
1239 SW Broadway Ave
503-222-9070
higginsportland.com

HOURS: Mon-Fri 11:30-12am,
Sat-Sun 4pm-12am

Higgins is a tranquil, secluded island in the stormy ocean of dining trends. This restaurant doesn't make waves by being au courant, with things like ramen bowls or beer cocktails, but by serving Northwest fare made with local ingredients, like oysters on the half shell, salmon, braised lamb with wild mushrooms, risotto with peas and bacon, and housemade charcuterie with pickles. When chef-owner Greg Higgins opened the restaurant in 1994, he was one of the first chefs in the city to focus on cooking with local, sustainable ingredients.

His love of all things local extends to craft beer (Hair of the Dog, *see page 58*, brews the "Greg," an organic beer made with kabocha squash, in his honor). But the restaurant's refined, globetrotting bottle list reveals an important acknowledgement: sometimes, fresh local food is wonderful with imported beers. Be sure to ask the beer "sommelier" for a suggestion.

While eating at the restaurant usually calls for reservations, the attached bar is there for a quick beer and a nibble. Tin ceiling tiles and a gleaming wood bar create an English pub-like atmosphere for everyone from Kindle readers to lunching co-workers. Expect uncommon imported beers on tap that are served in appropriate glassware.

PSST!
Chef/owner **Greg Higgins** commutes by bike to and from Hillsdale, something he's done since the early '80s.

INSIDER SIP
The Santa Rosa-brewed **Russian River** sour ales are almost always on tap here.

PARK IT
There are two bicycle staples by the building, and signposts otherwise for locking. No outdoor seating.

SW

▣ Goose Hollow Inn
1927 SW Jefferson St
503-228-7010
goosehollowinn.com

HOURS: Sun-Thurs 11-12am,
Fri-Sat 11-1am

One of Portland's saltiest and most welcoming institutions, Goose Hollow is the kind of place where old men play cards, smoke cigars (on the deck only, of course) and complain about the weather while toddlers rummage through a toy bin. Bud Clark, a former Portland mayor and the model in the famous "expose yourself to art" poster (there's one hanging in the bar if you don't know what we're talking about), opened the place in 1967 and named it after the surrounding neighborhood.

Among the dark wood, dazzling disco ball and framed memorabilia of Portland's history, you'll find a pleasant selection of beers on tap that range from PBR to Double Mountain one-offs served in 20-ounce pints. While many corners of the food menu are intriguing, we always order the Reuben, one of the best in town. This sandwich has the perfect ratio of meat to bread and enough melted Swiss to produce those crispy edges that make grilled cheese sandwiches worth eating. The standard side of carrot sticks helps justify the indulgence.

PSST!
Bud Clark commuted to City Hall by bike in the '80s, and the highest membership level of the **Bicycle Transportation Alliance** is the "Bud Clark Society."

INSIDER SIP
Upright Brewing's Goose Hollow Golden Ale is usually served here and only occasionally at Upright.

PARK IT
Unfortunately, there is no bike parking, but you can use the MAX station railing across the street in a pinch. There's outdoor seating.

SW

3 Bailey's Taproom
213 SW Broadway Ave
503-295-1004
baileystaproom.com

HOURS: Mon-Fri 2pm-12am,
Sat 4pm-12am, Sun 2-10pm

Amid the chugging buses, dinging MAX trains, historic hotels and high-rise office buildings, downtown has long felt lonely to the craft beer lover. But along came Bailey's Taproom and voilà: some of the best company ever. Bailey's has 20 rotating taps of fine craft beer with an Oregon emphasis, all of which are carefully detailed on an electronic screen behind the bar. The screen will help you make some good decisions; it shows precisely how much remains in a keg, as well as a beer's ABV, price and appropriate glassware.

Obsessively over the top? Maybe. But the screen represents Bailey's best traits: a crazy amount of beer beta. Though only if you want it. It's easy to simply drink a pint of whatever and read the *Willamette Week* without talking to anyone about platos or yeast strains.

The bartenders here are bona fide beer geeks, but they are willing to introduce patrons to beer basics, especially through taster trays. So sit back among the exposed brick walls and double-story windows to drink the perfect beer for your mood.

SW

PSST!
Order Mexican food from **Santeria** restaurant across the street, and have them deliver to your table.

INSIDER SIP
Events here, including **BelgianFest** and **CellarFest**, always have a spectacular lineup of beers.

PARK IT
Bike corral across the street and a couple staples near the outdoor seating.

SOUTHWEST UNDRESSED

Extras

BONUS STOP (FOR BAILEY'S)
Tugboat Brewing Company
711 SW Ankeny St
503-226-2508
d2m.com/Tugwebsite

HOURS: **Tues-Wed 4pm-12am,
Thurs-Fri 4pm-1am, Sat 5pm-1am**

Yes, Tugboat is a tiny brewery, and
no, it doesn't boast the city's best
beer. But Tugboat's most notorious
beer is the cloying **Chernobyl Stout**.
With 13% ABV, each patron is limited
to ordering two half-pints of Chernobyl
per visit. However, the brewery's
literary ambiance will win you over
with plenty of old books, low light
and board games. Make this a rainy
afternoon destination, even if you
forgot your elbow-patched sweater.

PARTY ON WHEELS
BrewCycle
971-400-5950
brewcycleportland.com

HOURS: **Book Online**

Imagine you and 14 of your
friends pedaling a bar down the
street from brewery to brewery.
That dream can become a reality
on the BrewCycle, a mobile
music-blasting party that rolls
on the city's west side. Costs run
$20-25 per person for a guided
tour or $150 per hour to rent.

RAISING THE BAR
Clyde Common
1014 SW Stark St
503-228-3333
clydecommon.com

HOURS: **Mon-Fri 11am-3pm & 6-11pm,
Sat-Sun 5-11pm, late night hours vary**
HAPPY HOUR: **Mon-Fri 3-6pm, Sat-Sun
4-5pm**

David L. Reamer Photography

Clyde Common is the kind of
place we'd expect to find in Oslo,
or any other chic Euro city. The
open space is always boisterous
and filled with beautiful people,
even late at night, and the food
and cocktails never disappoint.
Order anything from the regular
menu at the bar, such as popcorn
dusted with pimenton or cavatelli
with sausage and leg of rabbit.
Then ask bartender Jeffrey
Morgenthaler for something
along the lines of a barrel-aged
Negroni cocktail or the younger,
non-aged "Broken Bike," a bubbly
bottled mixture of Cynar, white
wine and lemon oil.

SW

FOOD CARTS

In Southwest, three major pods, conglomerations of food carts, rule the scene:

**Alder Street pod
SW Alder and Washington St
between 9th and 11th Ave**

**Original downtown pod
SW 5th Ave between Oak
and Stark St**

**Portland State University pod
SW 4th Ave between Hall
and College St**

HOURS: **Vary by location**

Do not leave Portland without trying at least one of the city's famed food carts. Don't worry, you have options. The city's 500+ food carts serve everything from authentic empanadas to wafflewiches stuffed with Nutella and whipped cream. You may find the random cart in an empty parking lot or between buildings, but cart "pods" offer the chance for the most window shopping.

David L. Reamer Photography

Our favorite downtown cart is Nong's Khao Man Gai, which serves a simple, but unforgettable, Thai poached chicken and rice. Located in both the PSU and SW Alder St pods.

TO GO

**John's Market
3535 SW Multnomah Blvd
503-244-2617**
johnsmarketplace.com

HOURS: **Mon-Fri 7am-10pm, Sat-Sun 8am-10pm**

Photo: Oliver

Nearby neighbors may go here for groceries, but the rest of us trek from all over the city to buy beer. The selection includes more than 800 types of beer in bottles and cans, on shelves and in coolers (plus some kegs). Check out the beer list on their website for inspiration.

SW

IN THE BEGINNING

Hillsdale Brewery & Public House
1505 SW Sunset Blvd
503-246-3938
mcmenamins.com

HOURS: **Mon-Thurs 11-12am, Fri-Sat 11-1am, Sun 12-11pm** | HAPPY HOUR: **Daily 3-6pm and 10pm-12am**

Photo: Liz Devine

Photo: Liz Devine

We can credit Portland's current beer scene to a handful of entrepreneurial beer lovers, especially brothers Mike and Brian McMenamin. Mike opened the beer-centric pub Produce Row Café with friends in 1974, before brewpubs were legal. That led him and Brian to open the Hillsdale Brewery & Public House, Oregon's first post-Prohibition brewpub. In 1985, the pub brewed its first beer, which may have been the still-standing Terminator Stout or Ruby Ale.

Since then, McMenamins has become a Pacific Northwest institution, with more than 60 locations in Oregon and Washington. Many many locations are historic properties, including a former funeral parlor and a schoolhouse. Adding to the quirkiness of these locales, their decorations include historical photos and whimsical artwork. Some McMenamins have restaurants and movie theaters while others run hotels and music venues. But the original Hillsdale spot is a simple place for drinking beer that's still brewed in a copper kettle.

SW

NORTHWEST ROOTS

New Crew, Old Brew

If you want to understand the roots of Portland's craft beer scene, put on a spiffy outfit, stand up straight and prepare to meet the parents. The city's Northwest quadrant holds the origins of craft brewing in this town. It also has high-density neighborhoods, making bicycling one of the sexiest and most efficient modes of getting around...and the most fabulous way to get your beer on.

SPOKES
"The car-free span of the Northwest's Steel Bridge supports a multi-modal mass: walkers, skaters, and cyclists galore!"

RYAN HASHAGEN | CHIEF TRICYCLE WRANGLER PORTLAND PEDICABS

SUDS
"Many people think of the NW as inaccessible, but there are lots of great places that offer affordable pints in a laid back atmosphere."

PAUL KASTEN | SOUS CHEF AND BEER STEWARD WILDWOOD RESTAURANT & BAR

The area now known as the Pearl District has long housed Portland's brewing pioneers, from Henry Weinhard to BridgePort Brewing, Portland Brewing Company and Widmer Brothers. Today in the Pearl District, spray tans and small dogs are as common as tattoos and backyard chickens in the Southeast. What was once a light industrial area is a now chic neighborhood where Portland's posh swing their Prada bags and look askance in their Ray-Bans. While fashions fluctuate dramatically here, and on neighboring NW 23rd Ave, beer remains a constant. A handful of breweries faithfully steep, dry hop and boil all manners of brew, just like the old days.

NW

NORTHWEST ROOTS
Bike Lowdown

BEER ROUTE | 2.9 MILES, EASY

Wearing a skirt or smart button-down shirt would be appropriate on this short route through Trendville. Because you don't get a lot of saddle time, this ride encourages lollygagging, drinking before 5pm, noshing in the sunshine and kissing in the park. Don't laugh too hard at cars stalled in traffic or searching for parking.

NW 13th Ave (*mile .5*) looks like an alley of loading docks equipped only to handle electric dolly traffic. Instead, the street chaotically channels cars, bikes and people past its stylish stores and sardine parking. The frenzy is its beauty.

For a true Northwest Portland experience, take the **NW 23rd Ave** side route (*at mile 1.6, go straight for two blocks instead of turning left*), which will bring you past high-end boutiques and busy cafes. These hot spots might convince you to lock up for a cool minute to join the throngs of window shoppers.

Jamison Square (*mile 2.4*) is the Northwest quadrant's most awesome urban park, with public art, kids running wild in the fountain, hipsters slumped nonchalantly on benches and little scrapes of green space. Recommended for kick-back chilling.

Other highlights: the bicycle boulevard on **NW Johnson** (*mile 1.8*) and the wicked **Pacific Northwest College of Art** bike parking corral. (*mile 2.3*).

NEED SOME KNOBBY?
As the largest wooded natural area within a U.S. city's limits, **Forest Park** provides many miles of vehicle-free woodsy delight. This 5,100-acre forest snugs right up to the Northwest neighborhoods. In one moment, you're under a quiet canopy of trees, and ten minutes later you can be drinking a chai at a coffee shop. You'll need a cross or mountain bike to navigate **NW Leif Erikson Dr**, the non-technical gravel road (*10.7 miles*) that snakes through the acreage.

Fat Tire Farm (*fattirefarm.com*, 2714 NW Thurman, rentals $40-125 per day) can hook you up with bike rentals and maps of the park.

NW

EXTENDED BIKE NERD ROUTE | 26 MILES, MODERATE-DIFFICULT | 1670 FT GAIN

NW Skyline Blvd earns its name. This road traces the undulating ridge between Portland Metro and the eastern reaches of the Willamette Valley. Sometimes this handsome stretch of road will shroud you in thick forest, and other times it will expose marvelous vistas. Sound nice? Oh, you will work for it. And it will be worth each pedal stroke.

Cloud Grazing on NW Skyline Blvd

RIDE GIST
You work hard to achieve ridgeline views and a remote roller coaster descent. **Moderate-difficult**.

PULL OVER
Skyline Tavern *(mile 8.1)* Embrace your Harley-lovin' self. Pint on the back patio?

BEST VIEW
NW Skyline Blvd: the name says it all.

Climbing to **NW Skyline Blvd** on **NW Cornell Rd**, use the paths around the two tunnels *(mile 1.3 and mile 1.7)*, the safest, most pleasant way.

NW Thompson Rd *(mile 3)* is a wooded, low-traffic sustained climb with a couple of steeper pitches where you prove your mettle. Cyclists routinely use this road for training.

The section of **NW Skyline Blvd** rocks the bucolic scenery and valley views.

NW Newberry Rd *(mile 10.9)* seems fashioned for lovers of descent. This remote, twisty road offers glimpses of volcanoes and the river valley. P.S. Don't eat it on the hairpin turns at the bottom.

On your return, you have three miles in the generous bike lane on busy **Hwy 30** before crossing the **St. Johns Bridge** and merging with the **North Portland Beer Route** *(mile 9.2)* to head back to Northwest via the **Broadway Bridge**.

WHEEL GREMLINS
You might spy a traffic sign with a symbol of an unhappy cyclist biffing on light rail tracks. (We once were riding with someone who ate it on the tracks right next to one of these signs. Hilarious, we mean horrible.) Point being, MAX and streetcar tracks crisscross the city, especially the Northwest, and are a hazard to cyclists. Be careful. Try to hit the tracks as perpendicularly as possible with your wheels.

NW

NW BEER ROUTE
Cue Sheet

0.0 START From ⭐ **Pints**, head west on **NW Flanders St**

0.3 LEFT NW 11th Ave

0.4 CHEERS!/RIGHT **2** **Deschutes Brewery/ NW Davis St**

0.5 RIGHT NW 13th Ave

0.8 CHEERS!/LEFT **5** **Irving Street Kitchen/ NW Johnson St**

0.9 RIGHT NW 14th Ave

1.0 CHEERS! **3** **BridgePort BrewPub**

1.1 LEFT NW Overton St

1.6 LEFT/CHEERS! NW 21st Ave/ **4** **Wildwood Restaurant**

1.8 LEFT NW Johnson St

2.3 LOOK! **A** **PNCA's** awesome bike parking

2.4 LOOK! **B** **Jamison Square**

2.5 RIGHT NW 9th Ave

2.7 LEFT NW Flanders St

2.9 END/CHEERS! ⭐ **Pints**

EXTRAS:
6 **Oven and Shaker**
7 **Rogue Distillery**
8 **Henry's 12th Street Tavern**
9 **Fat Tire Farm**

Don't let the wheel gremlins get you! (*pg 83*)

BrewCycle party on wheels. (*pg 77*)

TO FOREST PARK

trendy third!

NW 23RD

NW

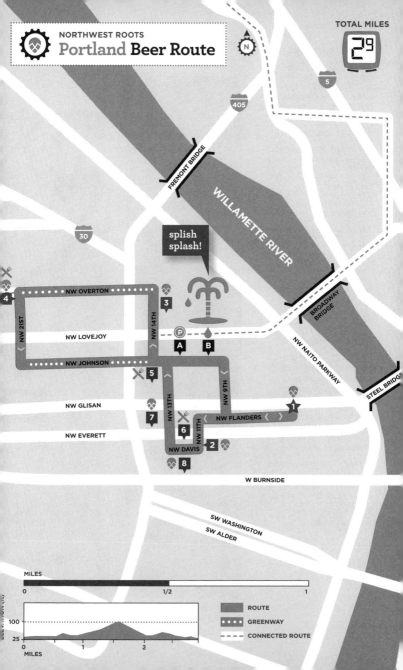

NW EXTENDED ROUTE
Cue Sheet

0.0 START ⭐ Leave beer route at **NW Overton St** and **NW 21st Ave**, heading west on **NW Overton St**

0.3 LEFT NW 24th Ave

0.4 RIGHT NW Lovejoy St, becomes **NW Cornell Rd**

1.3 VEER RIGHT Take bike lane around tunnel

1.7 VEER RIGHT Take bike lane around tunnel

3.0 RIGHT NW Thompson Rd

4.6 RIGHT NW Skyline Blvd

8.1 CHEERS! 1 **Skyline Tavern**

10.9 RIGHT NW Newberry Rd

13.0 RIGHT Hwy 30 (*unmarked*)

15.6 VEER RIGHT to 'St Johns Bridge"

16.0 LEFT Crossing St. Johns Bridge (*use sidewalk if you are nervous about traffic*)

16.8 RIGHT Hard turn at N Syracuse St; route connects with North Portland Beer Route at **N Willamette Blvd** (*Mile 7.9*)

*Take the North Portland beer route (*pg 21*) back to the **Broadway Bridge**, which shoots you into Northwest.

26.0 ENTER/END NW Portland

Riding the undulating hills of NW Skyline Blvd.

SAUVIE ISLAND

in the woods!

SAUVIE ISLAND BRIDGE

NW NEWBERRY

NW SKYLINE

NW GERMANTOWN

gnarly Harley!

ROUTE
GREENWAY
CONNECTED ROUTE
N BEER ROUTE (TO RETURN, pg 20)

NW

NORTHWEST ROOTS
Ride Stops

1 Pints Brewing
412 NW Fifth Ave
503-564-2739
pintsbrewing.com

HOURS: **Mon-Fri 11:30am-11pm, Sat 3-11pm** | HAPPY HOUR: **Mon-Sat 4-6pm**

As a coffee shop in the morning and a taproom in the evening, the only thing that could make Pints more Portland would be if it served Voodoo doughnuts and raised chickens (it doesn't do either, by the way). The myriad of commuters who stop here on the way to and from work most certainly are more enthused about drinking fresh beer than feeding squawking chickens anyway.

When Pints opens its doors in the afternoon, it becomes a beery oasis in the otherwise parched Old Town/Chinatown zone, with a nice selection of small-batch beers brewed on-site. While the mini brewery doesn't make beers with exotic

ingredients or do anything overtly sexy, like barrel aging, Pints makes consistently sessionable English-style ales, from an ESB to a red ale. The rotation changes frequently and a handful of guest taps help round out the selection.

NW

PSST!
Live music on Fridays and Saturdays livens up this quiet watering hole.

INSIDER SIP
The Steel Bridge Stout is delightfully creamy with a hint of dryness.

PARK IT
There's one bike staple on the whole block, but the metal fence across the street should work. Outdoor seating.

2 Deschutes Brewery
210 NW 11th Ave
503-296-4906
deschutesbrewery.com

HOURS: **Sun-Tues 11am-10pm, Wed-Thurs 11am-11pm, Fri-Sat 11-12am**
HAPPY HOUR: **Mon-Fri 4-6pm**

Deschutes Brewery is an import from the city of Bend, Oregon, which has a Portland-like ratio of locally brewed beer to bike fanatics. Deschutes opened the Portland brewing facility and pub in 2008, and almost immediately became a beer scene anchor.

Instead of the standard Pearl District industrial-chic interior design, Deschutes applied some Old World shellac with dark red walls, gilt-framed artwork and elaborate woodcarvings. The dining area is always humming, especially with families.

The pub only serves Deschutes beer, and some one-offs are poured here exclusively. Some of those beers are brewed on-site in the shining copper kettles visible through glass windows, but the bulk of Deschutes brews come from the larger Bend brewery. Classics include Mirror Pond Pale Ale and Black Butte Porter (one of Ellee's faves). But don't ignore the one-offs, which range from saisons to black IPAs, raspberry stouts, smoked wheat beers and gluten-free spiced golden ales.

PSST!
Deschutes is the fifth largest craft brewery in the country.

INSIDER SIP
There are always two beers on cask. Try the same beer on cask and from the keg to notice the difference, all in the name of beerducation.

PARK IT
There are custom bike staples all along the block. The brewery has outdoor seating.

NW

3 BridgePort BrewPub
1313 NW Marshall St
503-241-3612
bridgeportbrew.com

HOURS: **Sun-Mon 11:30am-10pm,
Tues-Thurs 11:30am-11pm, Fri-Sat
11:30-12am** | HAPPY HOUR:
Mon-Fri 4-6pm

Sometimes Portlanders seem like the people who mock celebrity-watching before buying a copy of *Us Weekly*. They grumble about million-dollar condos in the Pearl District, and wax poetic about how the neighborhood was once filled with starving artists and trash can fires, before heading out to enjoy the Pearl's welcoming parks, restaurants and BridgePort Brewing.

In 1984, winemakers Richard and Nancy Ponzi teamed up with brewer Karl Ockert to open one of the city's first craft breweries in a former rope factory, and the brewery's been pumping out beer ever since. In the mid-2000s the brewery underwent a renovation, and that's when the complaining began. Sure, the updated BridgePort feels a little sleeker and more family-friendly than the broody bar it once was. Gone are the cooks kneading pizza dough at the counter, but who can complain about the dramatic natural light flooding the industrial chic pub room? Gleaming stainless steel tanks behind the bar offer a hint of what happens in this large-scale brewery, but most brewing happens in tanks you can't see.

BridgePort is most famous for its balanced, floral IPA, which is always on tap. If you're lucky, at least one seasonal special will be on as well, such as Stumptown Tart, an annual release that includes various combinations of Oregon berries (two vintages were partially aged in oak barrels).

We always make a special trip to the brewery in October to try BridgePort's annual fresh hop beer, which is made with hops right off the vine from a farm about an hour outside of town. When you go, sit on the former loading dock—now an outdoor dining area—to properly savor Oregon's bounty.

NW

PSST!
Ask about limited edition barrel-aged beers. You never know what you might happen upon.

INSIDER SIP
Brewery tours run Saturdays at 1pm and 3pm if you'd like to see what happens behind the brick walls.

PARK IT
There are bike staples on NW Marshall St and deck seating (no bikes allowed).

4 Wildwood Restaurant
1221 NW 21st Ave
503-248-9663
wildwoodrestaurant.com

HOURS: Mon-Sat 11:30am-2:30pm,
Sun-Thurs 5:30-9pm, Fri-Sat 5:30-
10pm, Bar Hours: Mon-Sat 2:30pm-
close, Sun 5pm-close | HAPPY HOUR:
Mon-Fri 4:30-6:30pm

Without brew tanks or a ho-hum burger-and-fries pub menu, Wildwood doesn't scream beer. After all, it's a venerable Portland restaurant, the kind of place with top-notch seasonal ingredients, college students dining with their out-of-town parents and real estate agents celebrating West Hills home sales.

We love the fact that this elegant restaurant, replete with a swooping wooden ceiling and linen tablecloths, also has a top-notch selection of beer, including a "special and vintage" bottle list, which usually includes Russian River beers or an Alaskan Smoked Porter. Other beers in bottles include some of the Northwest's finest IPAs. Plus there are always four food-friendly beers on draft.

Bartenders and servers can recommend the perfect brew for your mood or meal. If you're not up for the formal dining experience, sit in the bar or at one of the outdoor tables, where you can nosh on Dungeness crab cakes served with shaved fennel, pan-fried Willapa Bay oysters and, yes, a burger. A really, really good one.

PSST!
Don't miss the happy hour, with $3 pints, fried corona beans and truffled popcorn.

INSIDER SIP
The deep whiskey list will please any connoisseur.

PARK IT
With just two bike staples nearby, the metal fence around the parking lot will work. They have outdoor seating.

NW

NORTHWEST ROOTS
❁ Extras

NIBBLES
Irving Street Kitchen
701 NW 13th St
503-343-9440
irvingstreetkitchen.com

HOURS: Mon-Wed 4:30-10pm,
Thurs-Sun 4:30-11pm, Sat-Sun
10am-2:30pm | HAPPY HOUR:
Daily 4:30-6pm

Irving Street Kitchen is a
refined slice of the South in
the heart of the Pearl District.
Think buttermilk biscuits and
ham with red pepper jelly,
smoked tasso jambalaya, or a
pork chop with artichoke and
parsnip hash. Hit happy hour
for Northwest wine, beer and
cocktail specials, plus great
small plates including ribs
with coleslaw and poutine.
No matter what time of day
(including during the killer
weekend brunch), count on
six reliable beers on draft and
Northwest wines from small
producers poured through a
custom tap-and-barrel system.

Photo: Courtesy of Irving Street Kitchen

SHARE THE LOVE
Oven & Shaker
1134 NW Everett St
503-241-1600
ovenandshaker.com

HOURS: Daily 11:30-12am
HAPPY HOUR: Daily 2:30-4pm,
Sun-Thurs 10pm-12am

If you've ever worked in a
restaurant kitchen, you know
what a cold beer can do for
morale. That's why the cooks
at Oven & Shaker let out a loud
cheer of appreciation every time
a customer orders the "Buy the
Kitchen a 6-pack for $6" (the
restaurant thanks the Publican
in Chicago for the idea).

TO GO
Most of Portland's larger
breweries, including a few in
the Northwest quadrant, include
mini shops: places to pick up
everything from a 22-ounce bottle
of a seasonal beer to a full-sized
keg. In case you left your bottle
opener at home, these shops
also sell plenty of accoutrements
emblazoned with brewery logos.

NW

GO LOCAL
Rogue Distillery and Public House
1339 NW Flanders St
503-222-5910
rogue.com

HOURS: **Sun-Thurs 11-12am, Fri-Sat 11-1am** | HAPPY HOUR: **Daily 4:30-6pm**

There aren't many places in the world with climates that foster barley and hops, two of the four primary ingredients in beer. Because Oregon is one of those blessed spots, Rogue

Ales, based in Newport, makes some uniquely homegrown brews using malting barely and aroma hops from Oregon farms owned by the brewery. These beers make up the "Chatoe" series, which express Oregon terroir. The whole array of Rogue brews, including the Voodoo Doughnut Bacon Maple Ale that pays homage to a Portland institution, are available on tap and in bottles at this outpost.

ON ICE
Henry's 12th Street Tavern
10 NW 12th Ave
503-227-5320
henrystavern.com

HOURS: **Mon-Thurs 11am-11pm, Fri-Sat 11-1am, Sun 10am-11pm**
HAPPY HOUR: **Mon-Thurs 3-6pm & 9pm-close, Fri-Sat 3-6pm & 10pm-close, Sun 10am-11pm**

If you've never seen an ice strip embedded in a bar that circles 100 beers on tap, now's your chance. Even though most Portlanders consider Henry's a tourist trap, you can't deny the selection or the opportunity to set your pint on a magical strip of ice that never melts.

IN THE BEGINNING
Beer has long been fermenting in the City of Roses. German immigrant **Henry Weinhard** opened a brewery in 1856 and brewed beer there until Prohibition forced him to switch to non-alcoholic beverages. Once beer became legal again, a series of mergers created the **Bliz-Weinhard Brewery**, which brewed beer in today's **Pearl District** until 1999. Today the **Brewery Blocks**, which house **Henry's 12th Street Tavern**, are named in honor of the century-plus of brewing.

In 1983, the Oregon State legislature made brewpubs legal, which launched a revolution. **Cartwright's** had been brewing since 1980, but the new law inspired some of Portland's most enduring brewpubs to set up shop, including **BridgePort Brewing** and **Widmer Brothers Brewing**, in the Northwest quadrant.

NW

The Hop in the Saddle Trio

Photo: Leah Nash

Over the years, these ladies became friends in true Portland style: at backyard barbecues, on the World Naked Bike Ride, at cyclocross races and over beers. It was only a matter of time before they realized they were destined to combine their professional super powers to create *Hop in the Saddle*.

LUCY BURNINGHAM is a writer who covers food, drink and travel for a variety of publications, including *The New York Times*, *Saveur*, *Bicycling*, *The Wall Street Journal*, the BBC, Lonely Planet guidebooks, *Sunset* and *Imbibe*. She's worked as a journalist for the past 12 years and holds a masters degree in nonfiction writing from Portland State University. Since moving to Portland in 2005, she's had numerous beer awakenings and now proudly grows hops for her rare batches of homebrew and seeks out stinky cheeses that were born to be savored alongside a good sour ale.

ELLEE THALHEIMER is an accomplished freelance travel writer and cycle tourist who believes that there are few better ways to travel and learn than by bike. Co-founder of the non-profit business alliance Portland Society, owner of Into Action Publications, zealous Oregonian, yogini, author of Lonely Planet's *Cycling Italy* and drinker of yerba mate, Ellee rarely turns down an adventure. Her most recent project was authoring and publishing *Cycling Sojourner: A Guide to the Best Multi-day Tours in Oregon*. When away from Portlandia, she misses the bejeezus out of her husband Joe and her puppy dog Winston.

LAURA CARY is a graphic designer who builds brands she believes in. After graduating from Rhode Island School of Design, she followed her wanderlust west where she began her career in San Francisco designing for clients ranging from bicycle companies to the opera. In Portland, Oregon, Laura founded Cary Design Group, a brand and identity firm. Portland has provided a welcome sense of community, bold entrepreneurial spirit and support of her love for the outdoors. Laura lives in North Portland with her husband, their son, two dogs and nine bikes.